INTRODUCTION TO HEALTH PROFESSIONS

Introduction to
HEALTH PROFESSIONS

Edited by

RUTH F. ODGERS, B.A.

Instructor and Assistant Director,
School of Allied Medical Professions, College of Medicine,
The Ohio State University, Columbus, Ohio

BURNESS G. WENBERG, M.S., R.D.

Associate Professor, Dietetics and Food Management,
The University of Washington, Seattle, Washington;
formerly Associate Professor, Medical Dietetics Division,
School of Allied Medical Professions, College of Medicine,
The Ohio State University, Columbus, Ohio

ILLUSTRATED

The C. V. Mosby Company
SAINT LOUIS   1972

CONTRIBUTORS

Robert J. Atwell, M.D.
Professor and Director,
School of Allied Medical Professions,
College of Medicine,
The Ohio State University

Philip Ballinger, B.A., R.T.(ARRT)
Instructor and Director,
Radiologic Technology Division,
School of Allied Medical Professions,
College of Medicine,
The Ohio State University

John W. Black, Ph.D.
Professor, Speech and Hearing Science,
Department of Speech Communication,
The Ohio State University

Marjorie L. Brunner, M.S., M.T.(ASCP)
Assistant Professor, Medical Technology Division,
School of Allied Medical Professions,
College of Medicine,
The Ohio State University

C. Kay Buckey, M.A., O.T.R.
Assistant Professor, Occupational Therapy Division,
School of Allied Medical Professions,
College of Medicine,
The Ohio State University

Robert J. Bullock, R.T.(ARRT)
Chief Radiologic Technologist,
The Ohio State University Hospitals

Clarence R. Cole, D.V.M.
Regents Professor, Veterinary Pathology,
College of Veterinary Medicine,
The Ohio State University

CONTRIBUTORS

Mae M. Davis, M.S.W., ACSW
Director of Professional Education and Inservice Training,
Medical Social Service Department,
The Ohio State University Hospitals

James P. Dearing, B.S.
Instructor and Associate Director,
Circulation Technology Division,
School of Allied Medical Professions,
College of Medicine,
The Ohio State University

William C. Dew, D.D.S.
Associate Dean, Secretary, and Professor, College of Dentistry,
The Ohio State University

Lloyd R. Evans, M.D.
Professor, College of Medicine;
formerly Vice Provost for Curricula,
The Ohio State University

O. Theodore Haaland, B.A.(ARIT)
Instructor and Director,
Respiratory Technology Division,
School of Allied Medical Professions,
College of Medicine,
The Ohio State University

Jack B. Hatlen, B.S., M.S., R.S.
Assistant Professor of Environmental Health,
School of Public Health and Community Medicine;
Director of the Office of Allied Health Programs
    for the Health Sciences Center,
The University of Washington,
Seattle, Washington

Katherine L. Kisker, R.N., M.S.
Instructor, School of Nursing,
The Ohio State University

David A. Knapp, Ph.D.
Associate Professor, Pharmacy Administration,
School of Pharmacy,
University of Maryland,
Baltimore, Maryland

James R. Kreutzfeld, B.F.A.
Instructor and Director, Medical Illustration Division,
School of Allied Medical Professions,
College of Medicine,
The Ohio State University

Thelma Lang, R.N., C.R.N.A.
Instructor and Director, Nurse Anesthesiology Division,
School of Allied Medical Professions,
College of Medicine,
The Ohio State University

Barbara K. Martin, B.S., R.D.
Instructor in Nutrition, Mount Carmel School of Nursing,
Columbus, Ohio

Barbara McCool, M.H.A.
Instructor, Hospital and Health Services Administration Division,
School of Allied Medical Professions,
College of Medicine,
The Ohio State University

James F. Noe, M.A.
Assistant to the Dean and College Secretary,
College of Optometry,
The Ohio State University

Daniel J. Pae, M.M., R.R.A.
Instructor and Acting Director,
Medical Record Administration Division,
School of Allied Medical Professions,
College of Medicine,
The Ohio State University

Mitzi Prosser, B.F.A.
Instructor, Medical Illustration Division,
School of Allied Medical Professions,
College of Medicine,
The Ohio State University

Nancy M. Reynolds, D.D.S.
Professor and Director, Division of Dental Hygiene,
College of Dentistry,
The Ohio State University

CONTRIBUTORS

Ellen Roller, R.N., M.P.H.
Formerly Assistant Professor,
School of Nursing,
The Ohio State University

Janice Sandiford, B.S., R.N.
Supervisor, School of Practical Nursing,
Columbus Public Schools,
Columbus, Ohio

Kathryn Schoen, Ph.D.
Associate Professor, Education and Speech Communication;
Associate Director and Associate Professor,
School of Allied Medical Professions,
College of Medicine,
The Ohio State University

Ethelrine Shaw, R.N., M.S.N.
Assistant Professor, Maternity Nursing,
School of Nursing,
The Ohio State University

James A. Visconti, Ph.D.
Assistant Professor, College of Pharmacy,
The Ohio State University;
Director, Drug Information Center,
The Ohio State University Hospitals

Burness G. Wenberg, M.S., R.D.
Associate Professor,
Dietetics and Food Management,
The University of Washington,
Seattle, Washington

Gladys G. Woods, M.S., L.P.T.
Associate Professor and Director,
Physical Therapy Division,
School of Allied Medical Professions,
College of Medicine,
The Ohio State University

Scott Worley, M.A., O.T.R.
Instructor, Occupational Therapy Division,
School of Allied Health and Social Professions,
East Carolina University,
Greenville, North Carolina

viii

PREFACE

Teachers and counselors in undergraduate colleges and secondary schools are faced with a difficult task as they strive to help students develop the background for making a sound vocational choice as well as for planning related education. In our complex and rapidly changing society, students are faced with the job of direction-setting rather than final choice. Their planning must involve careful appraisal of their aptitudes, interests, and values concurrent with an exploration of available opportunities.

This book is designed to provide educational and occupational information for a wide variety of health careers at a time when more and more young people are urgently needed in almost every area of health service. It is intended to show how the health professional functions in his job, what is necessary by way of education and training, and what opportunities for employment are available. It is hoped that it may prove equally useful as a textbook or as a resource for vocational counseling.

If the reader has caught the excitement and challenge of the opportunities available in modern health care, if he has gained a keener perception of the role of these health professionals, or if he is stimulated to explore further any of the occupations described as a step in his own vocational planning, the book will have served its intended purpose.

Almost all of the chapters in *Introduction to Health Professions* were originally written to supplement a survey course offered by the School of Allied Medical Professions, The Ohio State University. The course, designed to offer information about health careers, required the help and cooperation of many practitioner-educators to describe educational requirements, work performed, and career opportunities in the included professions. Students who used the chapters while enrolled in the course were asked to give suggestions and criticisms, and fellow health professionals were consulted as to the accuracy and relevance of the information.

Grateful acknowledgment is made to each of the contributing authors, to other professionals who offered suggestions and encouragement, and to the students for their helpful evaluations.

Acknowledgment is also due Miss Barbara Locher of the Occupational Therapy Division, School of Allied Medical Professions, for gathering and organizing information contained in the appendices and to Mrs. Dorothy Baker for typing and proofreading the manuscript.

Ruth F. Odgers
Burness G. Wenberg

CONTENTS

1 Factors influencing the education of health care professionals (Robert J. Atwell), 1

2 Medicine (Lloyd R. Evans), 9

3 Dentistry (William C. Dew), 21

4 Optometry (James F. Noe), 29

5 Veterinary medicine (Clarence R. Cole), 36

6 Nursing and related programs
Registered nursing (Katherine L. Kisker and Ellen Roller), 47
Nurse anesthesiology (Thelma Lang), 53
Nurse-midwifery (Ethelrine Shaw), 57
Licensed practical nursing (Janice Sandiford), 59

7 Pharmacy (David A. Knapp and James A. Visconti), 64

8 Physical therapy (Gladys G. Woods), 71

9 Dental hygiene (Nancy M. Reynolds), 79

10 Dietetics (Burness G. Wenberg and Barbara K. Martin), 85

11 Inhalation therapy (O. Theodore Haaland), 95

12 Medical record administration (Daniel J. Pae), 103

13 Medical technology (Marjorie L. Brunner), 109

14 Occupational therapy (Scott Worley and C. Kay Buckey), 119

15 Radiologic technology (Robert J. Bullock and Philip Ballinger), 127

16 Speech and hearing science (John W. Black), 135

17 Medical social work (Mae M. Davis), 144

18 Hospital and health services administration (Barbara McCool), 151

19 Medical communications (Kathryn Schoen), 158

20 Medical illustration (Mitzi Prosser and James R. Kreutzfeld), 167

21 Environmental sanitation (Jack B. Hatlen), 173

22 Emerging health professions (James P. Dearing), 179

APPENDICES

A Calendar of health careers, 191

B Professional organizations, 194

C Professional education and manpower supply, 197

D Estimated persons employed in selected occupations in 1967, 198

INTRODUCTION TO HEALTH PROFESSIONS

Chapter 1

FACTORS INFLUENCING THE EDUCATION OF HEALTH CARE PROFESSIONALS

Robert J. Atwell

Total health care in its modern concept must necessarily draw upon the personnel, techniques, and talents of a rapidly expanding range of disciplines. Those involved with establishing educational policies have increasingly come to recognize the need not only to fully utilize and enhance the skills of existing health professionals but also to attract greater numbers of dedicated people to existing programs. They have also seen the importance of developing new programs to keep pace with the technological and population explosions of the past decade. Education programs in the health sciences must be designed to provide personnel who have the skills that are most in demand, and these programs must prepare their graduates to make specific contributions as members of a health care team composed of personnel from many areas of the health sciences.

The factors that influence the kinds and numbers of health professionals needed also affect the number and variety of programs available for educating and training these personnel. An exploration of some of these factors is timely and important to those considering a career in one of the health sciences. (See Fig. 1.)

TEAM CONCEPT IN HEALTH CARE

The term "health team" is simply a figure of speech used to describe the groupings in which people work together to diagnose, treat, and rehabilitate the ill or injured. The implication of the term is that more than one person is necessary to provide optimal patient care.

At the turn of the century the three recognized health professions were medicine, dentistry, and nursing. Today, more than 200 health-related occupations have been identified. Within the hospital setting alone, there are approximately fifteen professionals,

1

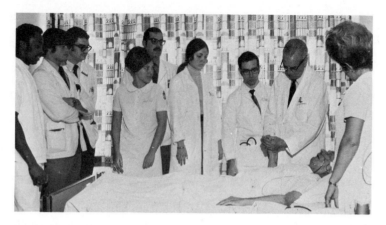

Fig. 1. The combined skills of many professionals contribute to modern health care.

technicians, and aides for each physician, all of whom make their specialized contributions.

Although it is an accepted fact that multiple input is essential to good patient care, the type of personnel used and the degree of their participation are decisions made by the physician. The makeup of the health team varies with the patients' needs, but certainly the physician and the nurse are constant members. Some health personnel are called upon more frequently than others, depending on the nature of the health problem and the degree of training and specialization of the staff. It is therefore of critical importance that the physician develop a real knowledge of what specialized personnel are available and how they can optimally be utilized. Only with this knowledge can he wisely choose the members of the team.

Although the number of workers available as opposed to the number of those in demand varies from one health occupation to another, increasing demands for all members of the health care team are creating career opportunities for service and stimulating the growth of many new educational programs.

ECONOMIC FACTORS

Economic factors certainly influence the health of a population, and conversely the health of a population also has a significant effect upon the economic stability of any country. Disease increases during war and famine. In fact, diseases such as tuberculosis have so decimated armies that wars have been lost. The health of a population improves during periods of prosperity; yet health care is frequently the first "luxury" sacrificed during a time of economic depression.

Many factors have been at work to change the relationship of economic status to health care. In the past the financial situation of individuals or families has usually determined the amount and quality of medical and dental care available to them. However, increasing incomes and prosperity have brought people to the conclusion that health care is no longer a luxury but a necessity— even a right. This attitude has been promoted by the armed services, the federal government, minority groups, and labor unions who incorporate health care provisions into their fringe benefit plans. Government funds administered through welfare programs, Medicare and Medicaid for the aged, and Project Head Start programs for the young have made health care benefits available to greater numbers of individuals. Various insurance plans, union welfare funds, and these government-supported programs have tended to remove the sharp edge from medical expenses.

COMMUNICATION FACTORS

The influence of communications on our population is quite awesome. Advances in radio, television, and other communications media have brought about a tremendous interest in and awareness of health. These various media have made our people health conscious through commercial advertising, health education, promotion of school health programs, and campaigns by voluntary health agencies.

However, increased availability of information does not necessarily lead to its general acceptance and use. The resistance to fluoridation of public water supplies is a case in point. Although they may accept the fact that fluoridation decreases the amount of dental caries, some groups believe that forcing a "medication" on the whole population is wrong in principle. Also, even though a person may know that smoking is deleterious to his health, he may continue to smoke, accepting the risks for the pleasure that he gets from it.

SOCIOLOGICAL FACTORS

Improved medical care has not only increased life expectancy but has also produced a redistribution of disease and illness among those over 65 years of age who are subject to the so-called degenerative diseases as well as among those of the younger population more subject to infectious diseases. Little progress has been made in the management of degenerative diseases, and although antibiotics have markedly affected the control of infectious diseases, success even in this area is by no means entirely satisfactory. Cultural and ethnic attitudes toward physicians, hospitals, and various types of treatments may still generate fear and superstition. Years ago people went to hospitals only as a last resort—they were places to which people went to die. Today, however, people turn to hospitals for the best treatment and speediest recovery from an injury or illness.

The growth of voluntary health agencies attests to the interest people develop for various reasons in the treatment of specific diseases. Drives to raise funds for research in leukemia, cerebral palsy, and muscular dystrophy are only a few of the activities conducted by these agencies. For example, the March of Dimes campaign to help children with birth defects has become a national endeavor.

SCIENTIFIC FACTORS

The knowledge explosion of the past several decades has had a profound effect. Prior to the 1930s, medical care consisted of limited surgical removal of abnormal parts and of symptomatic and nursing care. In less than forty years, specific treatments have been developed for specific diseases. Substitution therapy such as insulin for diabetes and cortisone for adrenal insufficiency as well as the sulfonamides and later the antibiotics for infectious diseases have completely changed the practice of medicine. The need for a specific diagnosis combined with technological advances and an increased knowledge of cellular chemistry have added test upon test, useful not only in the diagnosis but also in the management of the disease state. Improved anesthetic agents, the result of chemical and physiological research, have made it possible to perform surgical procedures that were unheard of fifty years ago.

Research supported by government grants has led to the development and testing of new drugs that were not even conceivable to our parents. The development of computers and the storage and retrieval of information obtained from seemingly unrelated investigations have resulted in unbelievable progress. Factual knowledge has increased so much in the last twenty-five years that simply finding needed material has become a major task.

POLITICAL AND GOVERNMENTAL FACTORS

Nearly everyone is concerned about good health and adequate medical care, and therefore this whole area has become an important political issue at the local, state, and federal levels. Thus government has played an increasingly larger role in the support, promotion, and direction of health care. The federal government assumed many health care responsibilities for its citizens during the depression of the 1930s and has provided increasing services for members of the armed forces through World War II and the wars in Korea and Vietnam. Veterans' hospitals, public health service hospitals, state and local departments of health, and boards of education have long taken an active interest in providing health care.

Let us look at the various laws related to health care that have been passed by the federal government in the last fifteen years. The addition of Medicare and Medicaid to the Social Security Act extends health care benefits to those over 65 years of age and to those under the age of 65 years who are considered to be medically indigent. The Health Manpower Acts and their amendments have been extended to include medicine, dentistry, osteopathy, optometry, podiatry, pharmacy, veterinary medicine, nursing, and the allied health professions. They have provided funds for the construction of facilities, basic support grants, special project grants, and traineeship grants to increase the number and quality of health professionals. The Regional Medical Programs have made large sums of money available to combat primarily the illnesses related to heart disease, cancer, and stroke. Comprehensive Health Planning emphasizes health care planning within the community. The establishment of the National Institutes of Health with support for research projects, the Hill-Burton Act for the construction of hospital facilities, and the Vocational Rehabilitation Act are all directly connected with health care. Certain other federal programs have also promoted health care in a less direct manner. The federal money involved in these programs represents many billions of dollars. The influence of this kind of spending on health institutions, research, and educational institutions has been profound.

TECHNOLOGICAL FACTORS

Some of the technological advances dealing with communications have already been discussed, but these by no means represent the major technological advances in medical care. The technological demands of World War II, the wars in Korea and

Vietnam, and the "space race" have produced numerous machines, gadgets, and instruments that have come to be considered essential in our health care institutions. To justify the cost of such instruments and to allow more patients to benefit from their use, the focus of treatment has shifted from the physician's office to the hospital. The automatic chemical analyzer, diagnostic and therapeutic x-ray machines, the electron microscope, the artificial heart, lung, and kidney are only a few examples of such equipment. Although many instruments markedly increase the number of diagnostic tests that can be performed, the burgeoning demand for more tests supports the need for further laboratory automation.

ACCREDITATION OF HEALTH EDUCATION PROGRAMS

Accreditation has been defined by the Office of Education of the Department of Health, Education, and Welfare as a process whereby an association or agency grants public recognition to a school, institution, college, university, or specialized program of study that has met certain established standards as determined by initial periodic evaluation. Accreditation has a direct impact upon the development of curricula for new programs in the health sciences. Accreditation of educational programs has been carried out under the aegis of the National Commission on Accrediting, which in turn has delegated responsibility for educational programs in the health sciences to the American Medical Association (AMA). The AMA often works jointly with other professional associations such as the American Physical Therapy Association. In the process of accreditation, educational programs are evaluated on the basis of minimal established standards, utilizing the "peer review" process to help assure that educational programs develop competent practictioners. Many of the newer health professions, however, have no formal accreditation process or are presently developing such a procedure within their own organizations. A national study of the accreditation process in the health professions is currently in progress under the auspices of the AMA's Council on Medical Education, the Association of Schools of Allied Health Professions, and the National Commission on Accrediting.

LICENSING, CERTIFICATION, AND REGISTRATION

Licensure of health care personnel is a function of the individual states, never of the federal government, and is intended primarily to protect the health and welfare of the public. Licensure originated at a time when there were few categories of health manpower and was thus initially designed to authorize physicians to perform all health care functions. As new categories of health professionals evolved and gained recognition, licensure was extended to define the area of competence to which each health care profession is limited. Thus licensure laws have gradually become mandatory and restrictive, although they do vary from state to state. The difficulty in changing laws pertaining to licensure and the fact that each state has different statutes have made for inflexibility. Such obstacles interfere with the growth of new areas of service and with manpower mobility. Among the licensed health professions are nursing, podiatry, physical therapy, medicine, dentistry, practical nursing, and nurse-midwifery.

Certification and registration are generally functions of professional organizations or groups of organizations. The concept of "peer certification" is widely used in this country. Certifying examinations are frequently used and represent an attempt to assure the public and the profession that a student has indeed been suitably trained by the educational program. Satisfactory completion of certifying examinations permits students to apply for registration by the professional organization representing their areas of specialization. Since licensure has not yet been extended to include many of the allied health professions, registration represents the only means of ensuring that professional personnel are capable.

Mention should be made of malpractice law since it relates to practice as defined by licensure laws. The tendency has been for health professionals to adhere to well-accepted and "safe" practices to avoid litigation. This tends to discourage innovation and change.

SUMMARY

The factors discussed and many more have contributed to an increase in (1) demand for medical care, (2) numbers and types of personnel needed, (3) specialization at all levels, (4) impersonalization in services, (5) government involvement, (6) enhancement of the health team concept, and (7) growth of educational and training programs for the health occupations.

Emphasis has shifted to include the "treatment of health," or preventive medicine, as well as specific therapy for specific diseases. Because the available diagnostic and treatment procedures available today are more complex as well as more effective, medical care requires more time of patients, physicians, and health team members than it did fifty years ago. The need for greater amounts

7

of information has resulted in specialization and a proliferation of types and numbers of health professionals. The diversity of diagnostic tests, specialization, size of facilities, and number of personal contacts have made the doctor-patient relationship seem very impersonal. However, medical care has improved vastly, even though interpersonal relationships may seem to have suffered.

Although it is always hard to predict the future, certain trends seem obvious. With the cost of inpatient hospital care rising steadily, the focus of health care will shift to the ambulatory or outpatient facility. Government will play an increasing role in health care. The need for coordinating the efforts of health care professionals will increase, and as the need for persons in health care delivery becomes greater, more and more educational and training programs at all levels will be developed.

BIBLIOGRAPHY

Darley, W., and Somers, A. R.: Medicine, money and manpower—the challenge to professional education. I. The affluent new health-care economy, New Eng. J. Med. **276**:1234, 1967.

Darley, W., and Somers, A. R.: Medicine, money and manpower—the challenge to professional education. II. Opportunity for new excellence, New Eng. J. Med. **276**:1291, 1967.

Forgotson, E. H., and Cook, J. L.: Innovations and experiments in uses of health manpower—the effect of licensure laws, Law Contemp. Prob. **32**:731, 1967.

Greenfield, H. I., and Brown, C. A.: Allied health manpower: trends and prospects, New York, 1969, Columbia University Press.

Kissick, W. L.: Health manpower in transition, Milbank Mem. Fund Quart. **46**:53, 1968.

Medical licensure statistics for 1968, Chicago, 1968, Council on Medical Education, American Medical Association. Reprinted in J.A.M.A. **208**:2083, 1969.

Selden, W. K.: Licensing boards are archaic, Amer. J. Nurs. **70**:124, 1970.

Chapter 2

MEDICINE

Lloyd R. Evans

PROFESSIONAL DEVELOPMENT

An account of the role of the physician in the delivery of health care should begin with a description of the development of medicine over the centuries. This is a comprehensive topic and within a limited space only some of the major figures in the development of this art-science can be mentioned.

The profession of medicine generally acknowledges as its founder the Greek physician Hippocrates, who lived in the fifth century B.C. He was the first to emphasize the casual relationships of disease and the symptomatic effects of the emotions. Prior to this time, people thought all ailments were due to the displeasure of the gods, and diagnoses and treatment were made by offering sacrifices to placate these deities. Because of Hippocrates, medicine took its first faltering steps toward the complex science that it is today.

A milestone in the development of medical science occurred in the middle of the second century A.D. Galen (Claudius Galenus), who served as physician to a troop of gladiators, was primarily interested in anatomy and wrote extensively on this subject. Because Galen based his hypotheses about human anatomy on the structure of lower animals, there were errors in his conclusions. However, his work was the accepted authority for the next 1,400 years and therefore had a profound influence on the practice of medicine.

Teachers referred to Galen with reverence until Andreas Vesalius seriously questioned his work. Vesalius, who lived from 1514 to 1564, corrected Galen's misconceptions of anatomy and was responsible for techniques used in the study of anatomy as we know it today. Many reproductions of his anatomical drawings can still be found in histories of medicine. Although he had a sense of humor and often showed skeletons standing in odd positions with their legs crossed, their hands resting on their own skulls, or holding spades as though they had just dug their own graves, the drawings are very accurate.

Almost simultaneously (1536) a French military surgeon, Ambroise Paré, developed techniques that enabled doctors to do surgery that could not have been otherwise performed. Prior to Paré's discoveries, open wounds were repaired by cauterization— searing with a hot iron or boiling oil. When a wound is cauterized, the bleeding is stopped, but a large amount of normal tissue is destroyed at the same time. Because dead tissue is a good medium for the growth of bacteria, infection often followed cauterization. Paré found that an application of certain ointments resulted in more rapid healing than did the use of cautery. He also developed a way to stop bleeding by tying a blood vessel with thread, a technique called ligation. There is much less shock following surgery using ligation than when cautery is employed.

In 1628 William Harvey, an English physician, published his first article on how the blood circulates. Harvey discovered that blood goes from the heart into the arteries, to the capillaries, into the veins, and back to the heart. Prior to this, it was thought that blood in the vessels oscillated back and forth but did not go through a complete circulatory process. There was no concept of a circulatory system, so no one realized that the same blood that circulates through the liver and the lungs, for example, also circulates through the brain, the kidneys, and the rest of the body. Until this discovery was made it was impossible to determine accurately how one organ influenced another. From this single discovery the science of physiology was born, and with it, the realization that the body is a series of integrated organ systems.

The discovery of the principle of vaccination in 1796 illustrates that not all important findings have been made in laboratories. Smallpox was then one of the great scourges of mankind. In the eighteenth century alone an estimated sixty million people died before a British country doctor named Edward Jenner discovered vaccination. Jenner noticed that milkmaids who had milked cows that had a disease called cowpox and whose fingers were thereby infected with this disease were subsequently unaffected by smallpox when this highly fatal ailment was epidemic in the area. He reasoned that the previous infection of cowpox had protected these milkmaids from the more serious smallpox infection. Cowpox produces a series of small pus-pimples on the abdomen of the cow. Jenner harvested some of this pus, put it on a patient's arm, scratched the skin and noted that the person subsequently developed one small pus-pimple such as we have all observed at our own vaccination sites. Later, those inoculated in this manner were free of smallpox, or immune, when an epidemic occurred. Even today, vaccination material is secured under laboratory conditions just as Jenner secured it, by harvest from the lesions of the abdomens of calves. Thus Jenner, who developed the concept of immunizing people artificially against this dread disease and so prevented the deaths of millions of individuals, became the founder of immunization.

Dr. William Beaumont (1785-1853) was a surgeon in the United States Army stationed at Fort Mackinaw on what was then the frontier and at other outposts in the Northwest. During this time he met and treated a French trapper by the name of Alexis St. Martin, who had a permanent opening through his abdominal wall into his stomach due to an old wound. Beaumont recognized this as a unique opportunity to study the physiology of digestion as it occurs in the stomach. These studies were the first of their kind ever performed, and later studies using sophisticated instrumentation have merely confirmed what Beaumont observed and published in his book *Experiments and Observations on the Gastric Juices and the Physiology of Digestion.*

Baron Joseph Lister (1827-1912) was a British surgeon who applied the teachings of Louis Pasteur, stressing the role of bacteria as the cause of infectious complications following surgical procedures. Also in the mid-nineteenth century an American obstetrician, Oliver Wendell Holmes, and a Hungarian, Ignaz Semmelweis, demonstrated that the deaths of many women following childbirth were caused by doctors who carried infection from one patient to the next because they did not scrub their hands thoroughly or sterilize instruments. Lister, Holmes, and Semmelweis stressed the importance of antisepsis and aseptic or sterile surgical and obstetrical techniques to prevent infection and death.

In spite of these advances, surgery was still difficult and hazardous because the intense pain often contributed to shock and death. Alcohol and paregoric were used as anesthetic agents, but they only slightly diminished the pain. Then in 1846 William Morton, a dentist at the Massachusetts General Hospital in Boston, demonstrated the use of ether as an anesthetic. Before an amphitheater packed with interested professional people, he removed a tumor from the jaw of a patient who had been put to sleep by the inhalation of ether. At about the same time Dr. Crawford Long of Jefferson, Georgia, also discovered the value of ether. These discoveries expanded the scope of medical care to a hitherto unimagined degree.

Another milestone occurred near the close of the nineteenth century when Wilhelm Konrad Roentgen discovered the roentgen ray. The application of roentgen rays, or x-rays as we call them, has unlocked the door to a whole range of diagnostic possibilities that were previously undreamed of.

The growth of medical knowledge has continued to accelerate at an even greater pace in our own century, and there are men of our time who will be immortal because of what they have done to ease human misery. Probably there is no more outstanding accomplishment than that of the British microbiologist Sir Alexander Fleming. Dr. Fleming, noting that bacterial colonies do not grow near mold, concluded that there must be something in mold that inhibits bacterial growth. Accordingly, he experimented using a common mold with the scientific family name of penicillin and identified the active substance that prevents bacterial growth, thus producing the first of the antibiotics.

Another medical landmark of this century was the discovery of insulin by two Canadian physicians, Sir Frederick Banting and Charles Best. They found that an extract of the pancreas provided a substance called insulin. When insulin is injected into patients with diabetes mellitus, they are able to properly metabolize sugar, which is otherwise impossible in this fatal disorder. The discovery of insulin set the stage for a host of advances in treating many of the endocrine malfunctions.

These discoveries have been so significant that since 1900 there has been a marked reduction in the mortality rate and more people live to be 80 years of age and older. Because of the vast amount of knowledge resulting from medical research, of which about half has been accumulated since 1960, doctors are committed not only to a lengthy period of training but to lifelong study as well.

From this brief historical account, it is clear that no single country has had a monopoly on medical discoveries. Medicine is an international discipline, and there has always been a free exchange of medical information among countries. Doctors make their discoveries available to all. It is highly unethical for a medical man to patent a discovery in order to prevent others from using it, unless he is employed by a pharmaceutical manufacturing house or other commercial firm that may patent his research discoveries.

DEVELOPMENT OF MEDICAL EDUCATION IN THE UNITED STATES

In colonial times the only physicians available were those ships' doctors who called at ports on the East Coast. If the patient could live with his illness until he could get to a port and wait for a ship to come in, he received treatment. This form of medical care was obviously less than satisfactory. Soon, young men began going to Europe for medical training, returning to the United States to set up practice. Charles Morgan was one of these early American medical men. He studied at Edinburgh, Scotland, and returned to Philadelphia where in 1765 he started the University of Pennsylvania Medical School, the oldest medical school in this country.

Because there were few university-based medical schools and because studying in Europe was both inconvenient and expensive, proprietary medical schools were founded. Four or five doctors would join together and give lectures to students who desired to study medicine. In addition, students might live in a doctor's home and work with him in his office. However, the number of students that could be trained in this fashion was limited. In the proprietary medical schools, students bought tickets for admission to lectures. Since professors received the money paid for the tickets and the most popular lectures were the best paid, there was considerable competition among members of the faculty to make their lectures attractive. Although this worked well in some schools, others were very substandard. Most medical schools were not connected with universities as they are today, and those without university affiliations were rather marginal operations.

In 1910 Abraham Flexner was employed by the Carnegie Foundation to study the educational practices of medical schools. After visiting every school, he wrote a report that shook medical education to its foundations. Overnight the number of medical schools decreased from more than 200 to 65. Those that disappeared were the small proprietary schools that lacked adequate libraries and laboratories as well as clinical facilities. Those that remained were greatly strengthened and emerged with professional postgraduate educational programs as we know them today. They have produced the scholars and clinicians who have given American medicine its place of leadership in the professional world.

MEDICAL EDUCATION TODAY

At the present time, students admitted to medical school have had three to four years of college, with the majority holding baccalaureate degrees. Most medical schools have four-year programs, followed by an internship during which the graduate has patient responsibilities for the first time. Internship is usually succeeded by an appointment to a residency in a selected specialty, a period characterized by greater patient responsibility and sophistication of learning. Appointments to residencies are from two to five years, a period that may be followed or interrupted by two years of military service. Not only are male physicians eligible for the draft until the age of 35 years, but there are fewer physical restrictions for a physician entering the service than for the usual draftee. Thus several years may elapse from the time when a man enters college until he enters practice. Many medical educators are anxious to shorten this long period of training by eliminating the internship and including this experience in the medical school curriculum. Some have also suggested admitting students to medical school after two or three years of college instead of waiting until they earn a degree. A few medical schools have combined the work required for both a baccalaureate and medical degree into six-year programs.

When an individual chooses the medical profession, he must carefully weigh the amount of time it will take him to achieve economic self-sufficiency. Although there are salaries for internships and residencies, they are not commensurate with those available to graduates of doctoral programs in other science areas. Many believe that this long period of economic dependence discourages some highly qualified individuals from applying for admission.

A high scholastic average is required for admission to medical school. There are probably few if any schools at which the grade average necessary for admission is lower than a "B."

More and more women are entering the field of medicine, but the rate of increase is slow. In some other countries a much higher percentage of medical students are female. In France, for example, 50% are women and in the Soviet Union the figure is even higher.

COSTS OF MEDICAL EDUCATION

The cost of medical education is a serious problem for many medical students. However, various sources of financial assistance are becoming more readily available to alleviate the problem. In addition to family assets and income, these include gifts, scholarships, grants-in-aid, fellowships, prizes, awards, stipends, and loans as well as the student's own earnings from summer employment and part-time employment during the school year. Because of the heavy study load and the accelerated pace of medical education programs, employment, particularly during the first year of medical study, is discouraged by most medical schools. Although summer employment provides both financial assistance and educational experience, students should be aware that in many medical schools there is a trend toward year-round curricula.

All medical schools are subsidized to varying degrees, so that the expense of educating a physician does not reflect costs to the student. According to the November 1970 issue of *Comments*, published monthly by the Chicago Medical School, estimates of the cost of educating a physician range from $5,000 to more than $30,000 per year.

Medical School Admission Requirements U.S.A. and Canada 1969-70, published by the Association of American Medical Colleges, states that total costs to students who are state residents attending their state school range from $6,196 to $13,180 for four years, the average being $9,688. For nonresidents, total costs range from $8,820 to $17,900, with an average of $13,707 for the four-year period.

Seventeen medical schools are currently participating in a federal study, organized under the auspices of the Association of American Medical Colleges and the National Institutes of Health, to more accurately determine the cost of educating physicians. This data should facilitate fund-raising and establish financial support patterns that will be of value to government, foundations, and private individuals seeking to support medical education.

NONSCHOLASTIC REQUIREMENTS FOR MEDICAL SCHOOL ADMISSION

There are important physical as well as psychological attributes that must be taken into consideration by committees that admit students to medical school. First is integrity. A man must be capable of honesty with himself as well as with his patients. Second is physical stamina. The practice of medicine is physically demanding of interns, residents, and practitioners. A medical student who had been an All-American football player said he found that medical school required more stamina than athletics. Third is emotional balance. This is difficult to judge since it must be determined from letters of recommendation, the applicant's autobiography, his medical history, and his poise at a committee interview. Emotional balance will be tested often under stress, even before the completion of training. Critical objective thinking, scientific curiosity, and a

Table 1. Major categories of medical practice*

Percentage of total physicians	Specialty	General description
17	General practice	
13	Internal medicine	Diagnosis and nonsurgical treatment of internal organs such as heart, liver, and lungs
9	Surgery	Diagnosis and treatment of disease, injury, or deformity by manual or operative procedures
6	Obstetrics and gynecology	Diagnosis and treatment of diseases of female reproductive organs and also care of women during and immediately following pregnancy
6	Psychiatry and neurology	Diagnosis and treatment of emotional disturbances, mental disorders, and organic diseases affecting nervous system
5	Pediatrics	Prevention, diagnosis, and treatment of children's diseases
3	Ophthalmology	Diagnosis and treatment, including surgery, of diseases or defects of eye
3	Pathology	Study and interpretation of changes in organs, tissues, and cells as well as alterations in body chemistry
3	Orthopedic surgery	Diagnosis and medical or surgical treatment of diseases, fractures, and deformities of bones and joints
3	Anesthesiology	Administration of various forms of anesthetic drugs necessary during surgical operation, diagnosis, or treatment
3	Radiology	Diagnosis and treatment of diseases through use of radiant energy, including x-rays, radium, and cobalt 60
27	Medical teaching, administration, research, and other nonpatient care activities	
2	All other specialties	

*From Horizons unlimited, ed. 8, Chicago, 1970, American Medical Association, pp. 49-51.

sincere concern for social problems are also highly valued attributes in the profession of medicine.

CAREER CHOICES IN MEDICINE

At the present time, approximately 17% of practicing physicians are general practitioners, but this percentage is shrinking. The remaining 83% are practicing in one of twenty major specialties. The major categories of medical practice are listed in Table 1.

A physician can become a specialist either by declaring himself to be one or by passing what is called a specialty board examination for certification in a particular field. A specialty board may require three to five years of hospital training, and some states also require practice experience before a physician is eligible to take the certifying examination. If he passes, he can declare himself to be a board-certified specialist. In many states there is no legal constraint to prevent a doctor, newly graduated from medical school, from hanging up his shingle the next day as a specialist in heart disorders or brain surgery. However, hospital regulations will prevent him from practicing as such until he has been certified by a specialty board. In twelve states it is not necessary to serve an internship prior to licensure by the state board.

There are roughly 300,000 doctors in the United States. Of these, 185,000 are in private practice, 55,000 are in institutional practice, 45,000 are in training as residents or interns, and about 15,000 are retired. There are many types of opportunities available in medicine. A doctor may practice by himself or as a member of a group. Such groups may be composed of doctors who all practice the same specialty, or they may form a clinic in which a variety of specialties are represented. Doctors may practice in the armed forces, in public health services, or in academic centers doing teaching and research. Some doctors work as hospital administrators or as officials in the medical departments of insurance companies or industrial firms.

Several major factors such as working hours, patient-visit rates, fee schedules, and professional expenses control the income of physicians in private practice. These factors may vary from year to year, from specialty to specialty, and certainly from doctor to doctor. Differences in practice setup, geographical location, length of time of practice, and amount of office help, together with the sophistication of training of such help, are all variables influencing income.

According to statistics for 1969 compiled by Medical Economics, Inc.,[1] incomes for physicians vary from the 9% who net $70,000 or more to the 25% who make less than $30,000 per year. Considering the net earnings among the five largest fields of medicine, 4% of general practitioners, 8% of internists, 6% of general surgeons, 8% of obstetricians and gynecologists, and 2% of pediatricians net $70,000 or more per year. At the lower extreme of the spectrum, 10% of general practitioners earn $10,000 to $20,000, while 5% of internists, 3% of general surgeons, 5% of obstetricians and gynecologists, and 12% of pediatricians earn amounts within this range.

The fields specified are the five largest, and specialists in these areas account for nearly two thirds of all medical doctors in the United States.

ACTIVITIES OF A PHYSICIAN

Statistics indicate that the average person sees a doctor five times a year. Obviously the chronically sick and elderly raise the average, while young, vigorous individuals hardly ever see a doctor. Because of an increased life expectancy, there is a higher incidence of the degenerative diseases such as arthritis and hardening of the arteries. The very young go to a doctor more often than those in their middle years and mostly for acute conditions. A mother may take her infant to the doctor's office for immunization several times during its first year. Sixty-six percent or more of a doctor's practice is focused on office visits, 10% on house calls, 9% in a hospital clinic, and only about 5% is devoted to caring for patients in a hospital. Some of a doctor's work is done over the telephone. Pediatricians, for example, commonly give advice on minor matters by telephone, particularly concerning the feeding of youngsters.

Seventy-five percent of those seeking medical care require diagnosis and treatment of a specific ailment. Eighteen percent go for a general checkup and 7% for immunization. The latter are mostly children. It is estimated that about 4% of the people receive 25% of the available medical services, while 12% of the people receive 50% of such services.

METHOD OF PRACTICE

How does a doctor approach the problems of a sick patient? First, he takes a medical history by directing questions to the pa-

[1]Medical Economics' continuing survey, Oradell, N. J., 1970, Medical Economics, Inc.

tient and listening carefully to the answers. There is a systematic way of doing this, touching not only on the immediate illness but on the past medical history as well. Second, he performs a physical examination using a stethoscope, ophthalmoscope, otoscope, blood pressure cuff, and other necessary instruments that increase his powers of observation. Third, he orders laboratory work, which usually includes a urinalysis, blood count, electrocardiogram, and x-ray films. The physician's diagnosis is then made on the basis of information obtained through these three steps. Approximately 75% of diagnoses are made on data derived from the medical history. Unfortunately, many people are reluctant to talk about their illnesses, and this deprives the physician of probably his greatest opportunity to make a correct diagnosis. About 15% of diagnoses are made as a result of the physical examination. The remainder are made as a result of laboratory findings.

Prevention, diagnosis, treatment, and rehabilitation are the four major tasks of a doctor. Because he is seeking relief, a patient's major concern is the effectiveness of treatment. However, the doctor's major concern is diagnosis, since he cannot treat a disorder correctly unless he knows what it is. For this reason a major part of medical education deals with making diagnoses. If the diagnosis is correct, the treatment is more likely to be appropriate and effective.

MEDICAL ISSUES OF OUR TIME

In addition to the problems presented by the individual patient, there are many important medical issues confronting physicians today. The philosophy underlying Medicare legislation indicates that Americans have come to view quality medical care as a basic right of every citizen. The recognition of this right and the needs it has generated have emphasized the serious shortage of physicians. In particular, the limited number of primary care physicians, family doctors to whom patients go first, has become an urgent problem.

Other major concerns result from the population explosion. One such concern involves existing laws regulating birth control and abortion. Another pertains to the patterns of population increases. Because there is a greater number of older people, there is an increase in the incidence of certain illnesses that used to be uncommon. However, the death rate due to infectious diseases is much lower.

We are spending 6% of our gross national product for health

care and related areas, and yet as a nation we rank seventh to thirteenth in some of the most important indices of health, for example, infant mortality and death from tuberculosis. We believe our medical system to be as good as that of any other country in the world, yet some nations that spend only 4% of their gross national product on health surpass us in such indices of health as those mentioned. Why do we have areas such as Appalachia where patients have trouble getting medical care or the inner city with the problems that abound there? Such concerns make it clear that the distribution and delivery of health care are our most important challenges as health professionals.

With recent advances in transplantation surgery, certain ethical problems have emerged that did not exist ten years ago. When is the donor of a heart considered dead in order that transplantation can be effected? When a hospital that has one artificial kidney has two patients needing help at the same time, who decides which patient should be put on the artificial kidney, knowing that the one who does not receive treatment may die? Physicians have always had difficult decisions to make, but some of today's problems are critical ones never faced before.

The spiraling cost of medical care is of concern to every one in the health field. The major increase has been in hospital costs, as wages of employees have been raised to levels more comparable with salaries in other fields. In some hospitals the cost of maintaining a patient in a four-bed hospital ward is over $100 a day. Who should pay for this? Can insurance carriers bear the load, or should there be a subsidy from the federal government? If people have the right to the best possible medical care, how will it be paid for?

These, then, are a few of the major issues in medicine today. Those who assume leadership roles in the health care system must seek answers to these questions. There is a critical need for more doctors and indeed for more health professionals of every kind. These professionals must be carefully selected and their education must be of the highest quality if the best possible health care is to be provided for the people of our country.

BIBLIOGRAPHY

Garland, J., and Stokes, J., III, editors: The choice of a medical career: essays on the fields of medicine, ed. 2, Philadelphia, 1961, J. B. Lippincott Co.

Horizons unlimited, ed. 8, Chicago, 1970, American Medical Association.

Howe, H. F., editor: The physician's career, Chicago, 1967, American Medical Association.

Chapter 3

DENTISTRY

William C. Dew

Dentistry is the profession that is concerned with maintaining the teeth and oral tissues in good health, preventing and treating dental diseases, and safeguarding the general health of the individual by detecting systemic disease in the oral tissues. It is a challenging profession that requires work with both the intellect and the hands. Dentistry affords the practitioner an opportunity to be artistic and skillful and offers independence, responsibility, authority, and opportunities for public service in a variety of situations.

HISTORY OF THE PROFESSION

The profession of dentistry shares a common origin with medicine. Many of the ancient medical documents and records have references to dental diseases and their treatment. Egyptian records dating as far back as 3000 B.C. include sections on the treatment of dental diseases, although there is no mention of the removal of teeth or their replacement. The Phoenicians (1600-687 B.C.) were the first to devise and record methods of replacing missing teeth and retaining the replacements through the use of soldered gold bands or rivets. Improvements in this art were made by the Etruscans (753-300 B.C.), who lived in central Italy, and by the Greeks (377-162 B.C.), the Romans (450-218 B.C.), and the Arabians (700-1200 A.D.).

The first records of the separation of dentistry from the profession of medicine date from the thirteenth to fifteenth centuries. Guy de Chauliac, a great surgeon of the Middle Ages, observed that operations on the teeth were properly the concern only of barbers and "dentatores." He made it clear that the "dentatores" of the fourteenth century were more than mere tooth pullers, for they treated diseases of the teeth and surrounding tissues as well as the scant knowledge of the time permitted. The treatments recommended were taken from the writings of Galen, an anatomist of the second century A.D., and from the Arabian writers. The emigration of Greek scholars to Western Europe during this period added much to dental and medical knowledge. Many of the contributors to the science of medicine also contributed much to dentistry—Vesalius, Fallopius, Eustachius, and Paré, to cite a few.

Pierre Fauchard (1690-1761) is considered to be the founder of modern scientific dentistry. His book Le Chirurgien Dentiste records the then current technical aspects of dentistry to which he contributed greatly.

John Hunter (1728-1793), an English physician, also wrote extensively on dentistry. Two of his best-known works are The Natural History of Human Teeth and A Practical Treatise on Diseases of the Teeth.

Dentistry in the United States had its beginnings in the latter part of the eighteenth century and was based upon the dental knowledge of Western Europe. John Boher, an Englishman, was probably the first competent dentist to practice in this country. Another was John Greenwood, who was dentist to George Washington.

Dental education in the United States had its beginning in Bainbridge, Ohio, under the guidance of John Harris, who was preceptor to his brother, Chapin B. Harris, and to James Taylor. These men later formed the first recognized colleges of dentistry in the United States.

The year 1839 is memorable in dental history for the establishment of a dental journal, the organization of a dental society, and the application for a charter to open a school for training dentists In 1840 the Baltimore College of Dental Surgery, the first of its kind in the world, opened its doors.

Rapid technical advances in dentistry occurred after 1850. Among these were the discovery of vulcanite as a denture base material; the development of gold foil, gold inlays, and amalgam as filling materials; the invention of the dental engine or mechanical drill; and the use of x-ray films and local anesthesia. Two dentists, Dr. Horace Wells and Dr. W. G. T. Morton, first used general anesthesia in 1846 and are credited with being among the first to use a general anesthetic agent.

Under the leadership of Dr. G. V. Black (1836-1915), who next to Fauchard is the best-known name in dentistry, dental education became truly scientific and professional. Dr. Black, who was Dean of the Dental School at Northwestern University in Chicago, performed brilliant research in anatomy and in the development of dental materials. He invented the foot-driven dental engine, and his classification of cavity preparations as well as many of his technical procedures are still used today.

After World War II, new advances in dental equipment (notably the air rotor), materials, research, and methods of practice made it possible for the dentist to be much more productive than before.

PROFESSIONAL DENTAL EDUCATION

The length of predental training varies from two to four years. A very few exceptional students are admitted after only two years. About half of all incoming students have completed three years of undergraduate study and the rest have completed four years, nearly all of whom have baccalaureate degrees. Many colleges have an arts-dentistry program in which the enrolled students attend a college of liberal arts for three years and earn a baccalaureate degree at the end of their first year in dentistry. Participation in this program makes it possible to earn two degrees in seven years. Predental students are encouraged to enroll in an arts-dentistry curriculum if it is available and are often given preference in admissions selection.

Required predental courses are kept at a minimum level. These include such areas as the following:

1. English composition and literature
2. Biology, including zoology
3. General chemistry, including qualitative analysis
4. Organic chemistry with laboratory
5. Physics with laboratory

It is usually recommended that predental students pursue a broad educational program that includes the social sciences and humanities rather than overemphasize the basic sciences, as many of these are covered in the professional curriculum.

The objective of dental education is to train a student to be knowledgeable and competent in basic sciences, dental laboratory procedures, clinical dentistry, practice management, and social and preventive dentistry. This is much to accomplish in four years; consequently, the program is rigorous and difficult, challenging and demanding. (See Fig. 2.)

Because of the nature of the dental curriculum and the physical limitations on the numbers of new students who can be accepted into dental schools, competition for admission is very keen. All students are required to take a dental aptitude test given by the Council on Education of the American Dental Association (ADA)

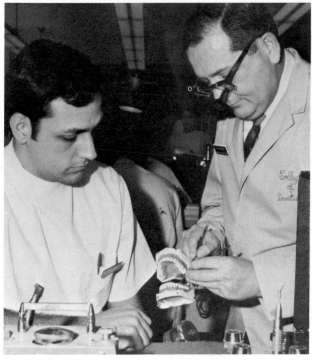

Fig. 2. Models of jaws and teeth are used in preclinical study to give students practice in instrument position and techniques.

at specific times at various testing centers. Admissions are based on predental academic performance, dental aptitude scores, and a personal interview.

During the third year of the professional curriculum a student is eligible to take the first half of the written examination offered by the National Board of Dental Examiners of the Council on Dental Education of the ADA. Toward the end of his final year he can take the second part of the examination. In addition, he must pass a clinical examination given by the state dental board of the state in which he desires to practice. Upon successful completion of this examination, he is permitted to practice only in that state. However, in some areas, regional examinations offer dentists who qualify a license to practice in each of several cooperating states.

SUPPORTING PROFESSIONALS

Most graduate dentists are engaged in private practice. In this situation a dentist or group of dentists has the responsibility for directing the activities of the office. The physical arrangement and facilities will vary with each office, but the modern trend is toward multiple operating rooms and several auxiliary personnel such as dental hygienists, dental assistants, dental technologists, receptionists, and office secretaries. The dentist who utilizes these additional personnel can be much more productive and provide better service to his patient than the dentist who conducts a one-man practice with little or no auxiliary help.

Training programs for dental hygienists are available at the college level. Not only are these professionals skilled technicians but they may also function as teachers in dental health education programs as well. They are becoming increasingly important in reducing dental disease. For the prospective hygienist who plans to work primarily in a private office, there are two-year professional training programs available, some of which award an associate degree.

For dental laboratory technicians there are vocational school programs at the post-high school level as well as on-the-job training in a dental laboratory. Enrollment in an approved training program provides one year of formal training and a second year of supervised training in a commercial laboratory and is an effective preparation for this career. The tasks of dental laboratory technicians include making and repairing such dental restorations as dentures, inlays, crowns, and bridges. Their objectives are to promote better health, greater comfort, and improved appearance, and they always work from the prescription of a licensed dentist. Salaries for the experienced laboratory technician range from $8,000 to $12,000 annually.

A third type of auxiliary personnel is the dental assistant, who may be employed by an individual dentist or by a group of two or more practitioners. There are increasing employment opportunities for assistants in clinics, hospitals, and other health agencies. Dental assistants are responsible for greeting patients and preparing them for examination, treatment, or surgery. They sterilize instruments, mix fillings, prepare solutions, and help the dentist to practice his skills. In smaller office situations they may also be responsible for such clerical tasks as making appointments, ordering supplies, sending out statements, keeping patient records, and answering the telephone. Many dentists are willing to select a likely applicant and give her on-the-job training. However, some dental schools, colleges, and junior colleges are offering training for dental assistants. Some programs offer an associate degree. Salaries for these workers range from $5,000 to $8,000 per year, depending upon community salary standards, extent of training, and amount of experience.

FUTURE TRENDS OF DENTAL PRACTICE

The emphasis in modern dental practice is increasingly being placed on prevention of dental disease and maintenance of oral health. With modern dental knowledge and procedures, it is possible to maintain the entire dentition in good health for a lifetime. There is also growing interest in and concern for the social aspects of dentistry. The goal is comprehensive dental care for all people. There is now such a large backlog of patients with extensive dental problems that it is necessary for the dentist to spend much of his time in the treatment of dental diseases. With currently available preventive measures such as fluoridation, dietary control, preventive treatment by the dentist, and adequate home care, it should be possible to vastly improve the oral health of our citizens.

CAREERS IN DENTISTRY

There are approximately 100,000 licensed dentists in the United States. About 6,500 are on the staffs of federal agencies (Air Force, Army, Navy, Public Health Service, Veterans Administration, Civil Service). Approximately 5,000 are engaged in dental education and research. The remainder are engaged in private practice. There are approximately 3,500 new graduates each year. When retirement and death of members of the profession are taken into account, it is evident that the profession is not likely to be overcrowded in the forseeable future.

Many graduate dentists continue their educational training and become qualified in one of the following eight recognized specialties of dentistry:

ENDODONTICS	Treatment of diseases of the internal soft tissues of the teeth
ORAL PATHOLOGY	Diagnosis of diseases or abnormalities of the oral cavity and associated structures
ORAL SURGERY	Treatment of diseases or abnormalities of the oral cavity and associated structures
ORTHODONTICS	Treatment of malocclusion and facial deformities
PEDODONTICS	Treatment of dental diseases in children
PERIODONTICS	Treatment of diseases of the supporting structures of the teeth

PROSTHODONTICS   Restoration of occlusion by replacement
of missing teeth

DENTAL PUBLIC HEALTH   Concern with dental epidemiology, biostatistics, and dental public health measures

With the exception of oral surgery, which is a three-year hospital-based program, these specialties require from eighteen months to two years of additional training.

The income of most dentists is well above average. Few dentists become wealthy, but most enjoy a very comfortable life. The *1968 Survey of Dental Practices* shows that the net income of dentists ranges from $17,558 to $27,614. The average yearly net income for specialists in those areas listed ranges from approximately $24,000 for the prosthodontist to more than $36,000 for the orthodontist. There is also a certain degree of prestige and respect afforded those dentists who are ethical in practice and have a genuine concern for their patients.

At the present time the energies of the dental profession are directed toward more sophisticated methods of practice, better delivery of dental services, prevention of dental diseases, and the community and social aspects of dentistry.

PERSONAL QUALIFICATIONS

The profession of dentistry is not suitable for everyone. The prospective dental student must have a good background in the basic sciences and the liberal arts. He must be industrious, intelligent, well motivated, and have a high degree of manual skill and artistic ability. He must have a concern for his fellow man and enjoy working with people. He must be a good businessman and office manager, and he should have an analytical mind and work well independently. Among the most important attributes are a good character and high moral and ethical standards. It is wise for a student who is seriously considering becoming a dentist to learn as much as possible about the profession by attending career programs, reading, and visiting dental offices and dental schools. This insight should help him to determine whether dentistry is the profession he should pursue.

The practice of dentistry is confining, demanding, and conducive to tensions. It requires a great deal of self-discipline, but most dentists would consider the rewards well worth these disadvantages. For the person who qualifies to become a successful dentist there can be no more rewarding or satisfying profession.

BIBLIOGRAPHY

Annual report on dental auxiliary education, Chicago, 1969-1970, Council on Dental Education, American Dental Association.

Annual report on dental education, Chicago, 1969-1970, Council on Dental Education, American Dental Association.

Dalton, V. B.: Genesis of dental education, Columbus, 1946, Spahr & Glenn.

Guerini, V.: A history of dentistry, ed. 1, Philadelphia, 1909, Lea & Febiger.

Lufkin, A. W.: A history of dentistry, ed. 2, Philadelphia, 1948, Lea & Febiger.

1968 survey of dental practices, Chicago, 1968, Bureau of Economic Research, American Dental Association.

Prinz, H.: Dental chronology, ed. 1, Philadelphia, 1945, Lea & Febiger.

The Ohio State University catalog, 1970-1971, Book 6, Columbus, 1970, The Ohio State University.

PROFESSIONAL ORGANIZATION WHERE FURTHER INFORMATION CAN BE OBTAINED:

American Dental Association
211 East Chicago Avenue
Chicago, Illinois 60611

Chapter 4

OPTOMETRY

James F. Noe

Optometry is the health profession specializing in the care of people's vision. Although modern optometry is a relatively young profession, its earliest foundations can be traced back to the Middle Ages. Like the other major health professions, optometry owes its present stature to a number of scientific discoveries and a series of contributing scientists.

PROFESSIONAL DEVELOPMENT

Visual care prior to 1300 A.D. was practically nonexistent. Spectacles had not been invented, and visual defects were merely tolerated. People suffering from "dimness of the eyes" were primarily thought to have an eye disease. They were considered to be useless members of society and were treated accordingly.

During the period between 1300 and 1900, astronomers, mathematicians, physicists, and other physical scientists made important contributions to the understanding of vision and the science of optics. Spectacle lenses were developed, and a limited number of people in the more technologically advanced nations were able to procure some primitive correction for their visual difficulties.

Additional optical knowledge and the founding of modern physiological optics led to the era of "modern optometry." The first training school for optometrists in the United States was established in 1892, and in 1901 the first state optometry licensing law was passed. The remainder of the states passed licensing laws in rapid succession, and the profession continued to develop.

Formation of state and national professional organizations, the increased number and quality of optometric training institutions, and the growing demand for and acceptance of professional optometric services served to enhance the growth of optometry as a vital health care profession.

PROFESSIONAL FUNCTIONS

The optometrist of the 1970s offers a variety of professional services. He provides comprehensive assistance to the public in maintaining and enhancing good vision and correcting vision defects. His work involves much more than merely correcting blurred vision, although this is an extremely important function. A number of diagnostic tests are performed by the optometrist to determine how the eyes of his patient focus and adjust to critical near and far distances. (See Fig. 3.) The eyes are a complex system, and people require different types of visual abilities to read a textbook, drive an automobile, pilot an airplane, or enjoy a movie or television.

It often takes an optometrist many hours over a number of months to provide the necessary services demanded even in routine cases. This health care professional is much more than a mere provider of eyeglasses. The optometrist must provide basic optometric services for every patient. The eyes must be carefully

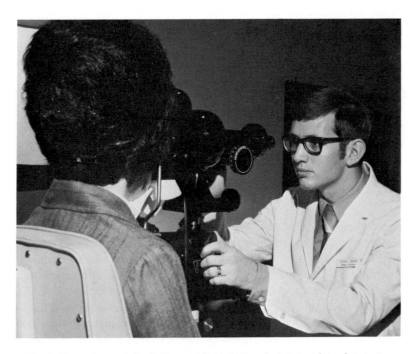

Fig. 3. One of a series of diagnostic tests is administered to determine the health and efficiency of the visual system.

examined for possible disease conditions. This requires the expert use of a number of scientific instruments and an applied knowledge of anatomy, physiology, and pathology.

Vision must be scientifically measured and a determination made of the patient's ability to use his eyes to see, focus, and aim with accuracy and comfort. These measurements and findings must then be carefully analyzed to ensure the most efficient solution to any vision problem that has been detected.

An exact set of instructions has to be prepared so the scientific and technical compounding of any corrective materials can be made by the laboratory. This finished prescription must then be carefully adjusted to the eyes of the individual patient to assure maximum results as well as comfort.

More complex cases call for more complicated testing. Problems in color vision, image-size measurements, binocular (or two-eyed) coordination, fields of vision, and depth perception are some of the more involved areas that demand careful testing by trained optometrists. Each of these areas requires specialized training, techniques, and equipment to reach accurate solutions to the patient's problems.

Many times it will be determined that prescription glasses are not necessary to solve a particular problem. The optometrist may prescribe visual training or orthoptics to remedy the diagnosed visual defect. These eye exercises must be carefully planned and explained to the patient to maximize their effectiveness. Often the optometrist will assist the patient in this treatment, using special scientific apparatus over an extended period of time. Such conditions as crossed eyes in children often lend themselves to this type of corrective measure.

Older patients present a different type of challenge to the optometrist. Correction of their visual problems often requires more than a single lens prescription. Specially designed bifocals, trifocals, or quadrifocals must be carefully prescribed to deal effectively with the needs of these patients.

The specialty of fitting contact lenses occupies a large segment of many optometrists' practices. The intricate measurements and careful fitting techniques required by this optometric service are challenging and time-consuming. Constant practice, study, and education are required to keep abreast of the latest developments. Ever-increasing numbers of people are selecting this type of visual correction, and the optometrist has the responsibility of keeping up-to-date in this rapidly changing area of specialization.

CAREERS IN OPTOMETRY

Most optometrists enter private practice. A majority of private practices have traditionally consisted of an individual optometrist assisted by one or more optometric aides. However, the present trend seems to be toward practices in which several optometrists with different areas of interest form a group practice, each contributing to a comprehensive optometric service.

There are various areas of specialization within optometry, in addition to the fitting of contact lenses. These include the examination and optical rehabilitation of aniseikonia, a discrepancy in the size of the images seen by each of the two eyes; the diagnosis and rehabilitation of problems involving binocular coordination and visual perception; the analysis and solution of visual problems associated with aviation, automobile driving, and other forms of transportation and with industry and schoolwork; and the correction of partial or subnormal vision. The goal is to help achieve clear, comfortable, safe, and efficient vision not only by optical means but also by making recommendations for enhancing the visual environment through better illumination, improved visibility of objects, and better design of equipment.

Optometrists are also employed by hospitals and clinics and by federal, state, and local agencies. A sizable number of optometrists serve as optometry officers in the Army, Navy, or Air Force or in the United States Public Health Service. Currently, graduate optometrists enter the Army and Air Force with the rank of captain and enter the Navy as lieutenants, junior grade.

Industry and government also employ optometrists in various research and development areas. For example, optometrists are involved in the National Aeronautics and Space Administration programs and in the work of major aviation companies as well as in the research projects of the larger optical manufacturing companies.

Optometrists are also needed to teach in colleges of optometry. Many of the colleges offer graduate programs in physiological optics for those optometrists interested in careers in education or research.

PERSONAL QUALITIES

Both men and women find optometry a rewarding career. An aptitude for and interest in science and mathematics coupled with a desire to be of service to people are the characteristics most important to an aspiring optometrist.

The personal satisfaction derived from rendering an important service combined with an adequate income make optometry an appealing health profession. An optometrist can determine his own office hours to best suit the requirements of his patients and family. Women optometrists find this flexibility especially attractive in combining a career with marriage.

The income of an optometrist depends on his professional skills and the services he provides. His income should equal that of the other professional men in his chosen community. Recent reports cite an average net income in excess of $20,000 per year for the established practitioner.

EDUCATIONAL PREPARATION

Present educational requirements for the profession consist of a four-year optometric curriculum preceded by a minimum of two years of specific preoptometry study. This preoptometry work can be completed at any accredited college or university, but the four-year professional training can be pursued only at one of the institutions accredited by the Council on Optometric Education of the American Optometric Association (AOA). There are presently twelve accredited schools of optometry located in the population centers of the United States.

Academic preparation for optometry should begin in high school with a college preparatory program in English, social studies, mathematics, science, and foreign language. Preoptometry curricula include courses in chemistry, physics, biology, psychology, and mathematics. Professional curricula embrace the various facets of the profession and include ocular anatomy, optics, psychology, and both the theory and practical application of optometric techniques. Students also spend a large part of their professional training in clinical settings. Under the supervision of the clinical staff, students work with patients to learn and refine the various skills so important in their future practice.

Upon successful completion of the professional curriculum, a student receives the Doctor of Optometry (O.D.) degree, which makes him eligible to take the state board examination required in every state for licensure to practice optometry.

OPTOMETRIC ASSISTANTS

The optometrist's role has been refined in recent years by the addition of auxiliary personnel in the area of clinical practice. Although exact job descriptions vary according to the size of the optometric practice and the type of services provided by the doctor, these assistants share certain general responsibilities.

Most optometrists employ an optometric office assistant. She is the doctor's "girl Friday" and serves as receptionist, office manager, and housekeeper. Her main tasks are scheduling daily appointments, preparing and filing patient examination records, billing, receiving fees, and attending to the details of operating an efficiently run professional office.

Most of the office assistant's training is received on the job, and her role is determined by her education and former experience. In addition, many optometrists encourage their assistants to attend periodic workshops and seminars sponsored by local and state optometry associations. These are often held in conjunction with state conventions and afford an opportunity for the assistant to update her knowledge of optometry office management, meet other assistants, and exchange ideas and procedures with them.

As an optometrist's practice grows, he may wish to employ an assistant to perform some of the more routine optometric tests. These assistants are referred to as optometric technicians, and their specific functions are determined by their education and experience in the area of optometry. The optometrist for whom the technician works carefully determines which diagnostic tests the technician can perform for a given patient to ensure an accurate vision analysis and diagnosis. These tests may differ from one patient to another and often need to be carefully supervised and validated by the optometrist himself.

A more exacting description of the optometric technician's role is presently being evolved, and training programs for technicians are being developed at a number of optometry schools. With the growing demand for more efficient health care at all levels for a rapidly increasing population, the optometric technician seems to be one answer to the problem of the shortage of optometrists in the United States.

FUTURE OUTLOOK

The complex demands made on vision by modern-day living create a steadily increasing demand for optometric services. As our population increases, so does the need for greater numbers of professionals in all areas of health care.

Numerous studies indicate that at present the 19,000 optometrists in the United States are not able to meet even the current need for services. Estimates of future needs are as high as an additional 1,000 graduates per year for the decade of the 1970s. Even with the newer methods of health care delivery being planned, there remains a critical need in all health professions for well-qualified, highly motivated men and women.

SUMMARY

Optometry as a profession has had a relatively short history. With the various services optometrists are now able to offer, the profession is beginning to realize its full potential as a part of the health care system. It is striving to meet the challenges of our growing population and the ever-increasing demand for quality health services. It offers a unique challenge to the student searching for a way to make a meaningful contribution to our complex society.

BIBLIOGRAPHY

Gregg, J. R.: Your future in optometry, New York, 1968, Richards Rosen Press.

Hirsch, M. J., and Wick, R. E.: The optometric profession, Philadelphia, 1968, Chilton Book Co.

Kitchell, F.: Opportunities in an optometry career, New York, 1967, Universal Publishing & Distributing Co.

PROFESSIONAL ORGANIZATION WHERE FURTHER INFORMATION CAN BE OBTAINED:

American Optometric Association
Vocational Guidance Department
7000 Chippewa Street
St. Louis, Missouri 63119

Chapter 5

VETERINARY MEDICINE

Clarence R. Cole

Veterinary medicine is concerned with the health and well-being of animals and man, the control of diseases transmissible from animals to man, and the discovery of new knowledge in comparative medicine. It has existed as one of the healing arts since prehistoric man perceived that the health of his animals was nearly as important as his own health. Records of ancient civilizations show some attempt to describe and treat illnesses of animals. Four thousand years ago an Egyptian papyrus recorded prescriptions for diseases of dogs and cows.

HISTORY OF THE PROFESSION

Nearly 200 years ago Benjamin Rush, physician and veterinarian, signer of the Declaration of Independence, and member of the Continental Congress and the medical faculty of the University of Pennsylvania, spoke of there being only one medicine.[1] He was pleading for one of the many causes he championed—the establishment of veterinary medical colleges in the United States. His plea went unanswered for nearly half a century, until the truth of his arguments became all too evident. Disease acquired from animals caused widespread human illness and death, and food shortages resulted from epidemics among food-producing animals. It was a truth that has been demonstrated throughout history. Tuberculosis, rabies, typhus, and many other diseases, some of man's most dreaded health threats, are passed from animal to man.

VETERINARY MEDICINE TODAY

Historically, veterinary medicine has come to the rescue of a disappearing food supply. Doctors of veterinary medicine, from those who guard the health of protein-producing farm animals to those who set and enforce standards for pure food from animal

[1]McKissick, G. E., Griesemer, R. A., and Farrell R. L.: Aerosol transmission of Rauscher murine leukemia virus, J. Nat. Cancer Inst. **45**:625, 1970.

sources, monitor the food-processing industry. Safeguarding our food supply by ensuring livestock health and the wholesomeness of foods of animal origin is one of the veterinarian's important functions. Through this work he directly serves the whole population.

The modern veterinarian, however, is responsible for a host of other safeguards—both to human and animal health—that are often simply taken for granted as part of the blessings of modern life. The control of rabies is a classical case in point. Anyone who has undergone the painful series of antirabies inoculations and knows that because of them he has been spared far greater suffering and certain death is not likely to dismiss lightly the veterinarian's contribution in this field. Fortunately, few of us fall into this category, thanks to the work of veterinarians. In 1945 over 10,000 cases of rabies in animals were reported, and thousands of people were treated with antirabies serum.[2] There have been only two reported human deaths from rabies in the United States since 1967. Its incidence has been decreased by 76% in the last fifteen years. Yet because rabies still persists in wild animals, veterinarians have the responsibility for vaccinating pets so that they cannot become a link in transmitting the disease from wild animals to human beings.

Because of their special knowledge of diseases that affect both animals and man, the work of veterinarians is essential to the control of zoonoses, one of the greatest concerns in the field of public health. Zoonoses are diseases transmissible from animals to man. Rabies is one of the zoonoses that no longer threatens human health because veterinarians have brought it under control in domesticated animals. Brucellosis (undulant fever) caused a loss of $90 million in livestock in 1947 but a loss of only $12.5 million in 1969 according to the United States Department of Agriculture. Its incidence in human beings dropped 94% in that time. In 1917 one in every 20 cattle was afflicted with tuberculosis and 125 per 100,000 deaths in human beings were attributed to the disease. In 1969 only one in 100,000 cattle had tuberculosis and the human death rate from this disease was reduced to 2.6 per 100,000.

In 1893 Dr. Theobald Smith, who was chief pathologist of the United States Bureau of Animal Industry in Washington, D. C., and Dr. F. L. Kilbourne, a veterinarian and director of the Veterinary Experimental Station of the Bureau from 1885 to 1894, published a

[2]Quarterly rabies summary, Washington, D. C., Oct., 1970, Department of Health, Education, and Welfare, United States Public Health Service.

paper, *Investigations into the Nature, Cause, and Prevention of Texas or Southern Cattle Fever.* In the paper the two doctors furnished the first proof that diseases can be transmitted by insects, something that had not been suspected until shortly before the turn of the century. Their discovery not only led to the eradication of Texas fever but provided the basis for Walter Reed's breakthrough regarding yellow fever in 1900.[3] Other researchers went on to discover the insect links, or "vectors," responsible for transmitting malaria, typhus, African sleeping sickness, and Rocky Mountain spotted fever from their wild animal reservoirs to man.

The list of diseases controlled through the work of veterinarians is impressive and may lull us into thinking that zoonotic study is a closed chapter in medical history. The facts are less reassuring. According to the World Health Organization, 30 of the more than 100 known zoonoses occur with some frequency in the United States. And these may shift insidiously because mutations in microorganisms can cause them to adapt to new hosts, possibly creating new zoonoses. Continual vigilance and alertness are needed to prevent them from becoming threats to human health.

In addition to old enemies in new disguises, diseases that were formerly found only in remote regions are being spread by the increasing convenience, speed, and volume of trade and travel and now are a worldwide threat to animal and human health.

Far from being exclusively concerned with animals, the veterinary medical profession today is oriented toward comparative medicine and the biomedical sciences. The veterinarian is in the forefront of space medicine and marine research, comparative pathology, and efforts to discover new and safe treatments for human and animal diseases.

Nearly every member of the veterinary profession, regardless of the branch of medicine in which he works, encounters disease conditions in animals that can contribute to an understanding of mankind's medical problems. Since veterinary medical training involves many animal species, it provides a particularly good background for studies in comparative medicine.

There are many ways in which the veterinarian combats both human and animal illnesses. Animal models of human diseases can be used for experimentation by veterinarians, who are familiar with both the animal and human forms of the disease. For example,

---

[3]Rapport, S., and Wright, R., editors: Great adventures in medicine, New York, 1952, Dial Press, p. 578.

swine, pigeons, and monkeys spontaneously develop arteriosclerosis, a disease that affects a high percentage of human beings and frequently results in heart attacks and strokes. Veterinarians are currently investigating leukemia in cats, pulmonary emphysema in horses, rheumatoid arthritis in swine, and aortic aneurysms in turkeys and are conducting experimentation vital to overcoming these diseases in human beings.

The veterinarian is responsible for research using laboratory animals, the indispensable bridge between theoretical chemistry and the use of new drugs on man himself. The laboratory animal industry is valued at nearly $500 million annually, and millions of dollars, for example, may be invested in a single stage of a research project involving germ-free animals of a given genetic type. But the expense and the effort are wasted if the animals carry a latent disease or a genetic factor that can distort the investigator's findings. Veterinary and other medical researchers depend on veterinarians in laboratory animal medicine to conduct investigations using high-quality standardized animals such as those that are germ-free. The development of the Sabin vaccine alone required fifteen years of research on 30,000 Indian and Philippine monkeys. Since this vaccine prevents poliomyelitis, we no longer need to close restaurants, swimming pools, and theaters during the summer in vain attempts to prevent the spread of this dread disease that killed and crippled thousands of people every year.

Veterinarians have played an important part in putting man into space by studying the reactions of animal subjects to high altitudes, acceleration, and deceleration. Their space research using monkeys and chimpanzees preceded manned space flight. In the manned space program a veterinarian heads the food and nutrition section that supplies the specialized space flight food, and another heads the radiological health team that is responsible for planning the evasion of radiation belts on space flights. A veterinarian was the first biological scientist to use lunar material in toxicological experiments.

Veterinarians are also working with marine mammals such as sea lions and dolphins to determine the effects of pressure and stress under water. Their findings will aid human aquanauts working at great depths in the sea exploring marine resources to help with the task of feeding mankind.

Veterinary medical research is essential to determine the effects of radiation on animals, ultimately to protect man. Veterinarians study the effects of both industrial nuclear energy and emergency radiation dosage to see how they affect the animal systems that man uses for food. Animal tests can also establish safe dosage levels for human beings.

We depend on veterinary toxicologists to determine the toxic potential of many chemicals, discover how they accumulate or dissipate in the environment, and evaluate their potential threat to man and animals The present severe shortage of these specialists could have alarming repercussions, since over three million chemicals are known and new ones are being synthesized at the rate of over 7,000 a year. Veterinarians conduct research using animals to determine whether newly synthesized compounds are useful for the treatment or prevention of disease in man. If a drug has therapeutic value, the veterinarians pursue their investigation to determine the dosage that can be safely administered.

Fortunately the acute shortage of veterinarians in the United States has not resulted in relaxing the standards of research relating to the discovery of new drugs for the treatment of human illness. In Europe in the 1960s, pregnant women who took the tranquilizing drug thalidomide gave birth to malformed babies who were missing fingers, hands, and feet. The shortage of veterinarians had made it impossible for the drug industry to conduct vital research on animals in order to determine the efficacy and possible dangerous effects of thalidomide before the drug was released for human use. The United States Congress, recognizing the shortage of veterinarians and the resulting tragic threat to human life, passed the Health Manpower Act of 1968 to provide funds to expand colleges of veterinary medicine through loans and scholarships for veterinary medical students and funds for facilities and educational improvement.

Dr. Luther Terry, Vice President for Medical Affairs of the University of Pennsylvania and also former Surgeon General of the United States Public Health Service, recently referred to veterinary medicine as being at a stage of scientific maturity and he stated that the profession was in a position to make its greatest contribution to human health and welfare. Some of the programs now being conducted by veterinarians have enormous implications for human health. Germ-free isolators and technology developed by veterinarians are now being used for burn patients. Some of the most promising investigative work on viruses as a possible cause of cancer is being done by veterinarians using germ-free technology. A new technique for repairing heart defects in animals may mean survival for human babies born with this defect. Research

Fig. 4. Alfie, representing the millions of pets for which the modern veterinarian is responsible, is shown with a favorite friend.

using germ-free animals at The Ohio State University College of Veterinary Medicine has enabled veterinarians to make discoveries related to virus-induced cancer and infectious diseases in animals.[4,5] The Stader splint, a metal bar with a steel pin at each end for insertion into the bone on either side of a fracture, was first demonstrated in early 1937. It is the invention of Dr. Otto Stader, a veterinarian from Ardmore, Pennsylvania. Spinal anesthesia was first developed by veterinarians, who were also the first to perform open-heart surgery and organ transplants.

In the field of animal health itself, veterinary medicine is responding to the huge growth in popularity of all types of animals kept as pets for companionship and pleasure. It has been recognized that pets make very definite psychological contributions to the mental health and well-being of urban man. There are an estimated sixty million dogs and cats in the United States now, and a projected estimate using a ratio of dogs and cats owned by the

[4]Rohovsky, M. W., Griesemer, R. A., and Wolfe, L. G.: The germfree cat, Lab. Anim. Care **16**:52, 1966.

[5]Smithcors, J. F.: The American veterinary profession, its background and development, Ames, 1963, Iowa State University Press, pp. 87 and 656.

Fig. 5. The modern veterinary hospital provides health services comparable to those available in the human hospital. Two veterinarians use a spectrophotometer to check the heart transmissions of an animal with a heart impairment.

present population indicates that there may be more than seventy-five million by 1980. (See Fig. 4.)

Horse racing is a billion-dollar business, and the number of pleasure horses is on the increase in every part of the country. Zoos now have more types of exotic animals, and more scientific attention is being paid to keeping them healthy and making it possible for them to reproduce in captivity. Doctors of veterinary medicine each year provide hospital medical services for many thousands of small and large animals, in addition to making many "house calls" via ambulatory services and caring for innumerable zoo animals.

In the field of animal health care, techniques and facilities are highly advanced. Since new surgical and medical techniques are discovered in animal research, veterinarians naturally use them on animal patients before they are made available to physicians for the treatment of human beings. (See Fig. 5.)

EDUCATIONAL REQUIREMENTS

The study of veterinary medicine requires a minimum of two years of preveterinary college study in areas such as biology, mathematics, chemistry, physics, animal science, English, and the humanities and social sciences. The first two years of most veterinary curricula involve the student in in-depth studies of those basic sciences that are required before he can go on to the study of clinical veterinary medicine. During the first year he studies the anatomy of the dog, cat, horse, cow, and other representative species as well as the principles of physiology, microbiology, and biochemistry. The second year is spent expanding his knowledge of physiology and introducing him to pharmacology, in addition to teaching him about the pathology of animal diseases.

The third and fourth years of the typical veterinary medical curriculum plunge the student into the practice of veterinary medicine through clinical studies in such areas as medicine, surgery, radiology, receiving, outpatient practice, farm practice, clinical pathology, public health, and preventive medicine. At the present time many veterinary colleges are working toward improvements in their curricula. As they do, most look carefully at the new curriculum initiated in 1969 by The Ohio State University College of Veterinary Medicine.

In this new curriculum the principles of comparative medical science are taught in the first two quarters. From the third quarter to the end of the third year, the core requirement for clinical medicine is taught by interdisciplinary teams, presenting an intensive study of animal disease on an organ system basis. Time is allowed for electives, since the faculty recognizes that knowledge acquired through individual choice and effort has the greatest value and the most permanence. During the fourth year, seniors study clinical veterinary medicine. They concentrate on specific clinical subject matter in preparation for a career in one of the various areas of clinical veterinary medicine.

The curriculum reduces the time necessary for the core courses and allows more time for electives. It also provides for an interdisciplinary approach to all subjects and offers maximum opportunities for independent study to permit the most effective possible use of student time.

REQUIREMENTS FOR LICENSURE

The Doctor of Veterinary Medicine (D.V.M.) degree is the only educational requirement for eligibility to take the national board examination for a license to practice veterinary medicine, dentistry, and surgery. Some states do not require those with sufficiently high scores on the national boards to take the state board examinations.

JOB OPPORTUNITIES

According to the Association of American Veterinary Medical Colleges, the licensed veterinarian will find his services in great demand. Each graduate of the class of 1970 had a choice of an average of nine known positions.

The shortage of veterinarians is already acute and is expected to get worse. Eighteen colleges of veterinary medicine supply the veterinarians for the entire country, and unless enrollment in these schools can be substantially increased, the nation will suffer a serious shortage of veterinarians by 1980. It is predicted that by 1985 the United States will have a deficit of more than 13,000 veterinarians.

More than half of all doctors of veterinary medicine join another veterinarian or enter their own private practice. Although more than half of the 26,000 veterinarians in active practice today are private practitioners, they cannot fill the widespread need for more veterinarians.

Increasingly, the new veterinarian is offered many attractive opportunities. The basic medical sciences such as anatomy, pharmacology, pathology, physiology, and microbiology offer masters' and doctors' degrees as preparation for careers in research.

The American Veterinary Medical Association recognizes veterinary medical specialties in public health, laboratory animal medicine, pathology, surgery, radiology, toxicology, and microbiology. Specialty areas require additional years of study. For example, to specialize in surgery it is necessary to complete an internship of twelve to fifteen months at a veterinary college or at a large private institution plus two years of residency training and two years of surgical practice for certification. The American College of Veterinary Surgeons, an arm of the American Veterinary Medical Association, is the certifying agency. There is a great deal of competition for the available internships. In 1969 there were sixty applicants for the ten positions open at the Animal Medical Center in New York.

Veterinary pathologists are certified upon passing an examination given by the American College of Veterinary Pathologists. They may take the examination not sooner than five years after receiving their D.V.M. degree. Three of those years must have been spent in pathology and two of the three in work with a board-approved pathologist.

Nearly half of today's veterinarians who are not self-employed work in the pharmaceutical, biological, and food industries or in government agencies. They conduct research to discover new drugs, vaccines, and food additives and test their safety and efficacy. Veterinarians in the military are responsible for the quality and safety of all foods served to the armed forces. Veterinarians supervise the inspection of all animals and animal products imported into the United States, and their vigilance has kept this country free of epidemics of serious foreign diseases for over forty years. The importance of this is illustrated by the outbreak of foot-and-mouth disease in 1967 and 1968 in Great Britain that resulted in the loss of 415,800 animals. Government veterinarians at both the state and federal levels work in wildlife, ecology, space, and nuclear medicine programs. Veterinary researchers work for hospitals, universities, or drug and pharmaceutical corporations to discover new treatments and surgical techniques applicable to both men and animals. Many veterinarians hold high posts in drug and pharmaceutical corporations.

The profession offers generous financial rewards. Graduating veterinarians going into industrial or government posts may expect an annual income of $13,000 to $18,000 at the outset, with subsequent promotions and raises according to the policies of the employer.

For private practitioners the initial investment in instruments and facilities is greater, but income is much higher and is limited only by the veterinarian's professional ability and managerial talent. The practitioner usually begins his career as an associate with an established veterinarian at a salary commensurate with those available in industry or government. After a period of experience and accumulation of capital, many young veterinarians will build their own animal hospitals and employ several veterinarians as associates.

Obviously, to call any of the many careers in veterinary medicine typical is an oversimplification, but since private practitioners are still in the majority, we might describe the daily routine in a small-animal practice.

On arriving at his hospital, the veterinarian might first make the rounds of his patients and then perform surgery until noon. In his afternoon office hours, he decides whether the animals brought in for treatment should be hospitalized or handled on an outpatient basis. He alternates evening ward checks and office hours with a partner. He is probably assisted by a receptionist who keeps patient records, a bookkeeper, a medical technician to help with laboratory work and surgical preparation, and one or more assistants on the wards of the hospital.

While the veterinarian in small-animal practice performs nearly all his work in his hospital and office, his counterpart in large-animal medicine is likely to use his laboratory and office mainly as a headquarters, maintaining radio contact while he drives from patient to patient. As with all professions, veterinary medicine demands a dedication to performing a needed service without regard for a fixed schedule. This is particularly true of the private practitioner, who must be available when emergencies arise.

Much of veterinary medical practice is devoted to preventing rather than curing disease. Pets receive immunizations in much the same manner as human babies and against as many diseases. The greater part of the large-animal practitioner's work involves diagnosis, vaccination, and consulting with animal owners as to nutrition, vaccination schedules, breeding programs, and all other aspects of herd management.

SUPPORTIVE PERSONNEL

The profession of veterinary medicine requires many types of supportive personnel. Colleges of veterinary medicine employ nurses, medical technologists, and medical illustrators as well as technicians who specialize in radiology, cardiology, electroencephalography, pulmonary function, and ophthalomology. They also hire medical librarians, medical record librarians, computer programmers, medical record administrators, and laboratory animal technologists. Private practitioners often employ assistants in one or more of these technical and supportive areas. The size of a private practitioner's staff will depend upon the size of his veterinary hospital. All supportive personnel have two factors in common: they are greatly needed by the veterinary medical profession, and they are allied health professionals working under the skillful direction and supervision of licensed veterinarians.

Veterinary medicine is in constant need of supportive personnel. The demands made on the veterinary medical profession, especially in the areas of research and animal care, exceed the available numbers of such personnel. Therefore opportunities for graduates in the allied health professions continue to increase, and competition for graduates is keen.

Chapter 6

NURSING AND RELATED PROGRAMS

REGISTERED NURSING

Katherine L. Kisker and Ellen Roller

HISTORICAL PERSPECTIVE

The real beginnings of nursing, contrary to popular belief, can be traced far beyond the mid-nineteenth century, for nursing is a profession that is almost as old as man himself. There are references to nursing in writings of the ancient Egyptians, Greeks, and Persians. In India, for example, there were training programs for nurses as early as 300 B.C. The word "nurse" is derived from the Latin word *nutrio,* which means to nourish and nurture, and these seem to have been the principal activities of nurses at that time.

Very little was done to improve the quality of nursing until the "Nightingale era" in the mid-1850s. In fact, in the early 1800s, nurses in European countries often had an unfavorable reputation and seem to have been concerned mainly with their own personal gain. Few had any real education. Florence Nightingale was a well-educated woman, although she had received only a few weeks of formal training in nursing. Deeply concerned with social and health reforms in England, she endowed a training school for nurses in that country and was instrumental in planning the curriculum and selecting the students. The changes she effected in nursing education emphasized a definite body of knowledge and practical experience for her students. The influence of her successful program spread throughout England and eventually to the United States, where in 1872 the first class of trained nurses was graduated from the New England Hospital for Women and Children in Boston. Nursing education began to move into the university setting in 1909, when the first collegiate school was established at the University of Minnesota.

Many social changes have occurred since the first nursing programs were developed in the United States, and these changes continue to have a great influence on both nursing practice and nursing education.

NURSES' CONTRIBUTIONS TO HEALTH CARE

Nursing practice involves several essential areas of patient care. Nurses are most frequently associated with physical care, for they provide or supervise the care that patients need because of illness or disability. This includes supplying what is necessary for the patient's safety and comfort as well as helping to prevent complications that may occur as a result of his illness or treatment.

A second function is that of providing emotional support. The nurse helps a patient to understand and to express his feelings about his illness and what it may mean to his everyday existence. This understanding may be strongly contributory to his recovery and rehabilitation.

The training and experience of registered nurses enables them to make observations that are invaluable in patient care. They generally are the only health professionals responsible for the patient on a twenty-four hour basis. The ability to perceive, recognize, and note facts concerning the patient's condition, to act on the basis of these observations, and to communicate them to appropriate persons on the health team may be critical to his recovery.

Nurses are also responsible for executing treatments that have been ordered by the physician. This requires a combination of technical skills and knowledge of the procedure, together with an understanding of its expected results.

Instructing patients and their families about an illness and the treatment measures used to combat it involves another important area of nursing. The instruction, whether planned or incidental, must be based upon the knowledge and previous experience of those receiving it. The nurse is sensitive to the most appropriate time for giving such information as well as to the manner in which it is given.

Another function is that of conferring with other health team members, the patient, and his family so that all patient services can be coordinated and so that all those involved work toward the same ultimate goal. Because they observe and interact with the patient, nurses are good sources of the information that other members of the health team need in order to make their most effective contribution to the patient's care.

Other important responsibilities of nursing practice lie in the areas of health maintenance and disease prevention.

EDUCATIONAL REQUIREMENTS FOR THE REGISTERED NURSE

The three types of programs that prepare students to become registered nurses are the diploma program, the baccalaureate degree program, and the associate degree program. The oldest and most common is the diploma program, which is sponsored by and situated in a hospital. Diploma programs are generally three years in length. In some instances they are affiliated with colleges where the students take basic science and liberal arts courses, while in other instances all instruction is given at the hospital school. These programs emphasize instruction and related clinical experience that focus on the care of hospitalized patients.

A second type of program is the baccalaureate degree program. Its graduates earn the bachelor of science degree. These programs are designed to give the student a broad general education as well as a specific knowledge of nursing. As most curricula are designed now, clinical nursing courses account for approximately half the credit hours. These courses provide opportunities for students to relate their knowledge of the science areas to actual patient care. The remaining hours of the program are drawn from the related humanities, the biological, physical, and social sciences, and electives. The programs vary in length from four to five academic years.

The third type of program is the associate degree program, offered through a community college, a technical institute, or a university. The program is two years in length and provides the student with a basic knowledge of the humanities and the social, physical, and biological sciences. The nursing courses include related theory and practice.

Admission requirements to schools of nursing vary. Although many schools require college preparatory work at the high school level, it is advisable to contact specific schools to determine their requirements.

The graduates of all three types of programs qualify to take a licensing examination. Graduates who pass these examinations are entitled to be licensed to practice as registered nurses. The requirements for licensure are determined by each state, and at the present time, all states are using the same examination.

Preparation for positions in teaching, nursing administration, and clinical specialties is available at the master's degree level. Graduates of diploma and associate degree programs must earn a baccalaureate degree prior to pursuing a master's degree.

49

A listing of the programs accredited by the National League for Nursing (NLN) can be obtained by writing to the League at 10 Columbus Circle, New York, New York 10019. This listing is also published in the organization's journal, *Nursing Outlook*.

JOB OPPORTUNITIES

Graduates of all three programs have a variety of employment opportunities. The extent to which nurses are able to assess a patient's needs, carry out nursing care, and function with other health professionals is determined by their own abilities and motivation, educational background, experience, and the policies of the employing agency.

Nurses are employed in a wide variety of settings. General hospitals employ the greatest number of nurses; within their confines the nurse may work in the emergency room, operating room, intensive care units, delivery room, nursery, patient care units, or in many specialized areas where nursing care is needed. Nurses may also work in outpatient departments, extended care facilities, clinics, doctors' offices, psychiatric care settings, schools, industries, public health agencies, and numerous other settings where health and health care are areas of concern. If nurses choose to be self-employed, they may become private-duty nurses and work in hospitals or in homes.

As members of the health care team, nurses work with many other health professionals. These include such personnel as occupational therapists, physical therapists, pharmacists, dietitians, and medical technologists. In circumstances where some of these professionals are not found but patients have need of their services, nurses may be expected to expand their technical skills to fill the gap. The only health team member with whom the nurse collaborates constantly is the physician. As health care becomes more and more complex, the nurse is becoming increasingly responsible for decisions that directly influence the well-being of patients.

The registered nurse not only works with people from other fields but also directs other nursing personnel who assist in giving direct patient care. These nursing team members include practical nurses, nurse aides, and orderlies or attendants. These individuals have training that ranges from the one-year course in practical nursing that qualifies the graduate to be examined for licensure to the on-the-job training of the nurse aides and attendants.

Continuing education as well as experience are essential for nurses who wish to develop and maintain a high degree of proficiency in their field. In other words, it is frequently through the process of gaining experience, reading the literature, and enrolling in workshops and conferences that nurses may become known as coronary care nurses, operating room nurses, pediatric nurses, psychiatric nurses, or community health nurses, to name only a few. Although basic skills are determined by the programs from which nurses graduate, competence and expertise develop through continuing education and experience within a specific setting.

Two of the areas mentioned, psychiatric and community health nursing, will be discussed in some detail to illustrate the means by which a nurse can enter such specialized fields.

Psychiatric nursing, sometimes called psychiatric–mental health nursing, provides nurses with the opportunity to contribute to the care of mentally ill people and to the promotion of mental health. The setting may be a psychiatric hospital, a mental health clinic, or a psychiatric unit within a general hospital. The primary skills needed in this type of nursing are interpersonal, as the nurse must be able to recognize and deal with the complexities of relationships between individuals and within groups. Nurses, psychiatrists, psychologists, social workers, and others often work in a team effort to help the mentally ill patient. Psychiatric nurses build upon their basic educational program by adding clinical experience and by participating in various forms of continuing education to become increasingly expert in this field.

Community health nursing, often called public health nursing, is part of the community's effort to meet the health needs of large groups of people. Community health nurses are concerned with communicable diseases, chronic physical and mental illnesses, health problems of mothers, children, and employee groups, and any other problems that are of concern to the population as a whole. The Executive Committee of the Division on Community Health Nursing Practice of the American Nurses' Association defines this area as a field of nursing practice that applies a body of knowledge and related skills in meeting the health needs of communities and of individuals and families in their normal environments such as the home, school, and place of work. It is an area of practice that lies primarily outside the therapeutic institution.

A goal of community health nursing is to help people maintain the highest level of health possible by promoting and teaching good health habits, working to prevent disease, and caring for and rehabilitating the sick and disabled. Nurses in this area may work with community service agencies to give generalized family service, or they may join the staffs of schools and industries. In generalized family service the health needs of all family members are studied and care and instruction are given. Community health nurses look at the dental, nutritional, safety, and other health practices of the individual family member and explore the relationships between family members—parent and child, husband and wife, and sick person in the family—to determine the effects of their interaction on the health of the family as a unit.

Community health nursing is a service given in cooperation with health, education, social work, and other professionals as well as with auxiliary workers and family members themselves. In this area, nurses may either take the lead in securing services for a family, or they may act as liaisons between the family and other workers. Community health agencies employ nurses who are graduates of baccalaureate, associate degree, diploma, or licensed practical nurse programs, and they also need auxiliary personnel who have health aide and/or homemaking skills.

Baccalaureate programs accredited by the National League for Nursing provide professional educational preparation for employment in community nursing. The graduates of such programs use a background of general education plus nursing skills, and from the field of community health they must add a knowledge of community organization, epidemiology, environmental health, vital statistics, and health education. Nurses with preparation in other areas are assigned responsibilities according to their educational backgrounds and may progress in community health nursing through staff development programs and actual experience. Most agencies provide opportunities for the continuing professional development of their staff through supervision, conferences, workshops, and other meetings at the local, state, and national level.

Master's level education in this area, in addition to preparation for supervision and teaching, helps nurse specialists to develop increased skill in providing family nursing services. In collaboration with others they are able to assess a community's health needs and determine what services should be developed on a community-wide scale. They may also consult with other staff members about family care and community needs.

The nurse works with other professionals and family members to assess the health needs of individuals, families, and the community. Planning to meet these needs and then implementing these plans are activities that must be coordinated with others. The family is the focus for much of this service, and the ultimate goal is improved family and community health.

Requests for this service come from family members, physicians, hospitals, clinics, teachers, social workers, and other community agencies and institutions. Nurses and community agencies actively seek referrals, for the early detection of disease facilitates control or prevention and enhances the health of the entire community.

The areas just discussed should not be confused with nurse anesthesiology and nurse-midwifery, two specialties that require additional education and for which certification is granted. These specialties are discussed later in this chapter.

NEED FOR NURSES

It is a commonly known fact that the need for health care professionals is skyrocketing. Nursing is no exception. In 1969 a total of 680,000 nurses were actively employed in the United States. At that time it was estimated that 200,000 more would be needed by 1970, with a total of 1,000,000 nurses needed by 1975. Over half of all professional people in health care occupations today are nurses. Many nurses who had retired because of family obligations are now returning to work on a part-time basis due to the critical need in most communities.

The salary scale for registered nurses varies according to geographical location, educational background, and the type of employing agency. In 1968 most beginning practitioners earned an initial salary of $5,000 to $8,000 per year. In 1970 the American Nurses' Association recommended $7,500 per year for beginning nurse graduates of associate degree and diploma programs and $8,500 a year for graduates with baccalaureate degrees.

Today, nursing is a flexible, far-reaching field that allows one to serve others in a variety of settings. There is a high degree of job security because of the great need, and work opportunities are available in almost any location.

NURSE ANESTHESIOLOGY

Thelma Lang

Nurse anesthetists are registered nurses whose advanced education and training qualify them to select and administer anesthesia. They are members of the operating room team whose principal concern is maintaining the life processes of the surgical patient, thus aiding the surgeon in his work and contributing to the comfort and welfare of the patient.

PROFESSIONAL DEVELOPMENT

During the last two decades of the nineteenth century, surgeons in Pennsylvania and Illinois began training nurses to administer chloroform and ether. This practice spread rapidly throughout the Midwest. By 1906 the total number of cases reported in which anesthesia had been used effectively by nurse anesthetists was 14,000.

During World War I the demand for anesthetists increased the need for training programs. The Army and Navy began training nurses as anesthetists, and many of them were active in ambulance corps and in base hospital units. American nurse anesthetists trained not only other American nurses in the field but some British nurses as well.

The number of schools of anesthesia increased in the 1920s, and local and state meetings of nurse anesthetists were organized, some of them based upon groups of training program alumni. In 1931 the organizational meeting for the American Association of Nurse Anesthetists (AANA) was held in Cleveland, Ohio.

When schools of anesthesia were evaluated on the basis of the criteria they used to determine their graduates' eligibility to take the qualifying examination, the need for an accreditation program became apparent. In 1946 an approval committee was established, and in 1952 the Board of Trustees of the AANA accepted the accreditation program recommended by this committee. Schools of anesthesia were notified of the minimum requirements for accreditation and were given one year to make any necessary adjustments. Revised minimum requirements adopted in 1962 included a training period of 18 months, 450 clinical cases with a total of 500 hours of clinical instruction, and 250 hours of class instruction.

The qualifying examination, first administered in 1945, is now given at more than thirty testing centers throughout the United States, and is administered by special arrangement in foreign countries. The number of schools training nurse anesthetists has increased from the fewer than thirty programs known to be in operation in the early 1920s to 201 in 1970.

RESPONSIBILITIES

Nurse anesthetists are primarily responsible for administering a prescribed anesthetic to a patient in the presence of and in accordance with the directions of either the surgeon in charge or the anesthesiologist. Their total responsibility is much more encompassing and includes an obligation to the patient, the surgeon, and to the operating room team.

Competence in administering anesthesia to the patient requires constant alertness and good judgment, and anesthetists must refrain from any acts that can adversely affect their competence. Nurse anesthetists, like other members of the surgical team, are personally liable for their actions, regardless of whether the surgeon may be jointly or primarily liable. They should hold in confidence all information of a professional or private nature.

Nurse anesthetists must earn the physician's confidence in

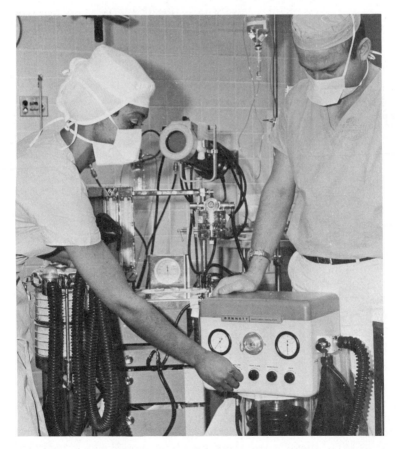

Fig. 6. It is important that all equipment be carefully prepared and checked out before anesthesia is administered to the patient. A student nurse anesthetist, under the watchful eye of a supervisor, prepares machinery to be used during neurosurgery.

their ability to competently and safely administer anesthesia to the patient. It is the anesthetist's duty to give the physician the sense of security that comes with knowing that the patient is in good hands.

The nurse anesthetist must make an effort to acquire and maintain the cooperation of the operating room personnel. Any problems should be explained to the operating room nurses so that the entire surgical team can work together. The anesthetist is part of a team, and it takes the concerted efforts of each team member —physician, anesthetist, and operating room nurse—to give the patient appropriate care. (See Fig. 6.)

Nurse anesthetists have a responsibility to continue learning throughout their professional lives. Membership in the AANA is an important means of accomplishing this, because it provides an opportunity to keep abreast of new developments and trends in the profession.

EDUCATIONAL REQUIREMENTS

Standards for evaluating the qualifications of nurse anesthetists have been established by the AANA. An applicant must be a registered nurse before entering an accredited school of anesthesia. The course of study, approximately eighteen months in length, includes such areas as the anatomy and physiology of the nervous, respiratory, circulatory, endocrine, and excretory systems. The physics of gases and the application of gas laws in equipment as well as methods and techniques for administering anesthetic agents are studied. The student must acquire a thorough understanding of ventilation and resuscitation, the pharmacology of anesthetic drugs, and the electronics of monitoring devices. Knowledge of these fundamental areas coupled with extensive clinical experience prepares the student for the qualifying examination. Satisfactory performance on this examination is a prerequisite for membership in the AANA. The salary for these specialists ranges from $800 to $1,500 monthly.

PERSONAL QUALITIES

Ideal nurse anesthetists are well-adjusted individuals, exhibiting high moral, professional, and ethical standards in their relationships with patients, co-workers, and employers. They approach the demands of anesthesia with skill based on knowledge and practice, and they possess inquiring minds that lead toward even higher levels of conduct and ability.

NURSE-MIDWIFERY

Ethelrine Shaw

The nurse-midwife is a registered nurse who has specialized in the care of mothers and infants throughout maternity cycles that are defined as normal according to established criteria. The knowledge and skills required for competent practice in this area must be acquired through programs recognized by the American College of Nurse-Midwifery. These programs are open only to registered nurses and offer academic preparation as well as clinical experience in all relevant areas of care. Criteria defining normal circumstances are established by individual agencies and institutions.

ROLE OF THE NURSE-MIDWIFE

Although nurse-midwives as nurses are concerned with health and have the knowledge, skill, and ability essential to providing good nursing care, their additional educational preparation qualifies them to assume more responsibility than registered nurses for the health care of women and infants during pregnancy, labor, and delivery and during the postpartal and newborn periods.

CONTRIBUTIONS TO HEALTH CARE

The nurse-midwife functions in any health care setting that offers services to women, infants, and families during the maternity cycle. Nurse-midwives may be found in any of the following settings and roles:

1. *The community:* In antepartum and satellite clinics the nurse-midwife may follow up normal patients on an independent basis. In other instances, nurse-midwives may serve as resources to the nursing staff and assume responsibility for in-service education. Their work may also include assessing patient needs, making follow-up visits to homes, and instructing patients.
2. *The hospital:* The nurse-midwife manages uncomplicated labors and delivers the infant. Follow-up care is given to mothers and babies during postpartal hospitalization. The nurse-midwife is also concerned with the general health needs of the family unit.
3. *Administration:* Nurse-midwives have opportunities to administer maternity or public health services.

4. *Schools of nursing:* Nurse-midwives who are prepared to teach may assume faculty positions in schools of nursing.

HISTORICAL PERSPECTIVE

Advances in health care have introduced many safeguards for both mother and infant—before, during, and after birth. In primitive societies, women delivered their own infants or were assisted by other women. Those who seemed the most skillful in handling childbirths and were willing to assist were set apart as midwives. The term "midwifery" means *with woman.* Another word that came into use after physicians began to practice midwifery is obstetrics, which is derived from the Latin term "obstetrix" and means *midwife.* Although the earliest writings on midwifery were by physicians, they were not read by the women who practiced midwifery. These women were generally illiterate and had no formal training to prepare them for their work. Physicians had some control over the practices of midwives, but they themselves were seldom involved except in difficult deliveries. Midwifery and those who practiced it were regarded as inferior by physicians.

Nursing and midwifery, however, are interwoven from an historical as well as from a futuristic point of view. As Florence Nightingale began to identify nursing functions and responsibilities, a system of educating nurse-midwives was also proposed.

Although nursing gradually became acceptable, midwifery in general continued to be a practice that was looked down upon in the more technologically advanced Western nations. During the early part of the century, women in the United States continued to give birth to their infants at home, using hospitals only in cases of emergency or during complicated births. Although it had become fashionable for the wealthy to have a physician in attendance to assist at deliveries, unknown numbers of women were cared for by untrained, unsupervised, and often newly immigrated midwives. Their lack of skill, together with inadequate scientific knowledge, adverse social conditions, and minimal prestige and power in the hands of women, were among the many factors that contributed to high infant and maternal morbidity and mortality rates.

By 1917 health care during pregnancy had been initiated for patients under the care of physicians, nurse-midwives, and non-nurse-midwives. This service was most significant in decreasing mortality and morbidity. In 1925 the Frontier Nursing Service, the first nurse-midwifery service in the United States, was started in Wendover, Kentucky. Such services soon proved that nurse-midwives could make significant contributions to the health care of mothers, babies, and entire families. In 1932 the Maternity Center in New York City established the first school for the educational preparation of nurse-midwives.

With the advent of more advanced and rigorous educational programs, there is increasing acceptance of nurse-midwifery as a specialty, and the stereotyped image of this professional has undergone many changes.

There are two types of programs that prepare nurses for this specialty. The first, ranging in length from six to eight months, awards a certificate in nurse-midwifery. The second leads to a master's degree and certification and requires from eleven to twenty months for completion. Current trends seem to favor this second type of program.

LICENSED PRACTICAL NURSING

Janice Sandiford

Within the health profession today, a special career is attracting qualified men and women. This career is practical nursing, and it appeals to the person who wants to be a nurse but who is not in a position to undertake the more extensive preparation or responsibilities of the registered nurse. Practical nurses are vital members of the health care team, supplementing the work of the registered nurse, physician, and other health personnel in caring for the sick and promoting community health. Licensed practical nurses find rewarding work experiences in hospitals, extended care facilities, private homes, public health agencies, offices, and clinics.

AVAILABLE TRAINING

Most programs in practical nursing are twelve months in length. Some programs in practical nurse education are offered by public school systems, usually as a part of a vocational school or adult education program. Others are offered by community colleges, technical schools, or private hospitals. Approval of schools of practical nursing is under the jurisdiction of state boards of nursing. Correspondence courses are not approved and their graduates are not eligible for licensing examinations.

Student tuition is set by the institution conducting the program and varies in accordance with the kind and amount of funds available for operating the schools. Fees plus the cost of all required materials as designated by the school are usually from $500 to

$1,000 for the year. Most programs are conducted for the benefit of local residents and therefore dormitory facilities are not available. Students should give careful consideration to ways of meeting living expenses before enrolling.

Financial assistance in the form of scholarships and loans is available for qualified applicants. Because many such funding programs are locally sponsored, it is necessary to consult the admissions officers of specific schools for detailed information.

PREENROLLMENT REQUIREMENTS

Educational requirements for admission to schools of practical nursing vary greatly. In some states the minimum requirement is an eighth- or tenth-grade education; however, many states are requiring a high school diploma or its equivalent for licensure. Passing the General Education Development (GED) test constitutes high school equivalency in most states and is recognized by most schools.

Some schools require that applicants have a background in science (general science and biology), mathematics, and English (vocabulary, grammar, and comprehension). Schools establish specific educational prerequisites to assure that the applicant will have a reasonable chance of completing courses satisfactorily. Since entrance requirements do vary among states and among schools within each state, the applicant should get specific information from the school he wishes to attend. Schools often require a preentrance examination to help in the screening-selection process. Successful work experience as well as references and a personal interview are also given consideration.

Men and women, married or single, are accepted as students. The age range for applicants is usually 18 to 50 years of age. There are some practical nursing programs in vocational high schools that enable students to earn a high school diploma and study practical nursing at the same time.

EDUCATIONAL REQUIREMENTS

Curricula stress experience with patients, and the student learns to deal with actual clinical situations early in the program. There is classroom study of basic nursing skills and related subjects such as body structure and function, nutrition, conditions of illness, sociology, and personal and community health. Minimum standards for curricula are established by the state board of nursing so that they conform to the state's nursing practice laws, and

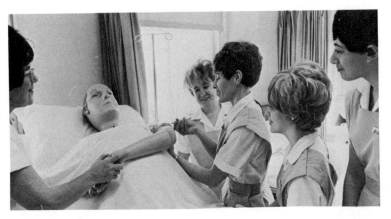

Fig. 7. Student practical nurses develop skills to be used later in clinical experience.

these standards must be met if the school is to receive board approval. (See Fig. 7.)

LICENSURE

Upon completion of the program in practical nursing, the new graduate is eligible to apply for licensure. Passing a licensing examination permits the graduate to legally use the term "licensed practical nurse" (L.P.N.). In some states, "licensed vocational nurse" (L.V.N.) is the accepted title. Examinations are scheduled at various times throughout the year and are conducted by state boards of nursing. Since 1968 all states have used the National League for Nursing Test Pool Examination.

ROLE OF THE LICENSED PRACTICAL NURSE

The role of practical nurses is defined by law in each state. In addition, each employing agency may have its own job description. It is generally agreed that the licensed practical nurse works in relatively simple nursing situations under the direction of a registered nurse, licensed physician, or dentist, performing specific duties in the care of the sick, injured, or infirm. In more complex nursing situations the practical nurse assists the registered nurse. A simple nursing situation is one in which conditions are relatively stable and critical judgments are not required. Practical nurses may perform only those procedures for which they have been trained. In addition, state laws define the areas of responsibility to which

61

practical nurses are limited. Since the governing of nursing practice is a state responsibility, the law varies from state to state.

EMPLOYMENT OPPORTUNITIES

Licensed practical nurses can find employment in any one of several health care areas. Most graduates work in hospitals as general or private-duty nurses. Positions are also avaliable in nursing homes, extended care facilities, clinics, doctors' offices, health departments, and the armed services. Opportunities are available to practical nurses in pediatrics, obstetrics, surgery, intensive or emergency room care, and many other areas. Practical nurses are on the job wherever there is a health need, and they are caring for people with many kinds of health problems. Salaries for the licensed practical nurse vary from place to place but generally are about three fourths of those earned by registered nurses.

The licensed practical nurse who wishes to practice in another state can apply for licensure by endorsement of that state. Since nursing laws vary somewhat from state to state, the applicant must meet requirements for licensure set by the state in which licensure is desired. There is enough similarity among state laws to make licensure by endorsement a rather standard process for the graduate of a state-approved school.

SUMMARY

Practical nursing is a promising profession for individuals interested in humanitarian service that requires dedication and offers rewarding experiences. Applicants are usually high school graduates between the ages of 18 and 50 years. The programs, approximately one year in length, include classroom study as well as clinical practice and are vocational in nature. They are relatively inexpensive.

A challenging position awaits the graduate upon satisfactory completion of the course and licensure examination. Practical nurses are needed everywhere in greater numbers.

BIBLIOGRAPHY

A.N.A. position on education for nursing, Amer. J. Nurs. **65**:106, 1965.

Blumberg, J. E., and Drummond, E. E.: Nursing care of the long term patient, New York, 1963, Springer Publishing Co.

Boone, P.: The nurse-midwifery service at Harlem Hospital Center, Bull. Amer. Coll. Nurse-Midwives **13**:13, 1968.

Breckenridge, M.: Wide horizons, New York, 1952, Harper & Row, Inc.

Cutter, I. S., and Viets, H. R.: A short history of mid-wifery, Philadelphia, 1964, W. B. Saunders Co.

Dietz, L. D., and Lehosky, A. R.: History and modern nursing, Philadelphia, 1967, F. A. Davis Co.

Facts about nursing, New York, 1969, American Nurses' Association.

Fox, C. G.: Toward a sound historical basis for nurse-midwifery, Bull. Amer. Coll. Nurse-Midwives **14:**76, 1969.

Heidgerken, L.: Nursing as a career. Is it relevant? Amer. J. Nurs. **69:**1217, 1969.

Novak, G.: Your career opportunities in nursing, New York, 1962, Rowman & Littlefield, Inc.

Nursing education programs today, New York, 1961, National League for Nursing.

Ross, C.: Personal and vocational relationships in practical nursing, Philadelphia, 1969, J. B. Lippincott Co.

Stewart, I. A., and Austin, A. L.: A history of nursing, New York, 1962, G. P. Putman's Sons.

Swenson, N.: The role of the nurse-midwife on the health team as viewed by the family, Bull. Amer. Coll. Nurse-Midwives **13:**125, 1968.

Task force on health manpower: health manpower action to meet community needs, Washington, D. C., 1967, Public Affairs Press.

The surgeon general looks at nursing, Amer. J. Nurs. **67:**64, 1967.

The training and responsibilities of the midwife, New York, 1967, Josiah Macy, Jr., Foundation.

Young, L. S.: Nursing's challenge, Nurs. Outlook **17:**62, 1969.

PROFESSIONAL ORGANIZATIONS WHERE FURTHER INFORMATION CAN BE OBTAINED:

American Association of Nurse Anesthetists
3010 Prudential Plaza
Chicago, Illinois 60601

American Nurses' Association
10 Columbus Circle
New York, New York 10019

National Association for Practical Nurse Education and Service
475 Riverside Drive
New York, New York 10027

National Federation of Licensed Practical Nurses
250 West 57th Street
New York, New York 10019

National League for Nursing
10 Columbus Circle
New York, New York 10019

Chapter 7

PHARMACY

David A. Knapp and James A. Visconti

The pharmacist is the most accessible of all American health workers. The pharmacy, his place of practice, may be found on almost any corner of any street in the country, and it has become a modern American institution. However, pharmacy is one of the most ancient of the professions. Since the dawn of history there have been men who have dedicated themselves to the development of drugs for healing and comforting the sick. Written prescriptions have been found that date from as early as 3600 B.C., and the Ebers papyrus, written about 1550 B.C., contains references to many chemicals, formulas, and cosmetics used at that time. In these years the professions of medicine and pharmacy were as one, and it was not until the Arabian period (700-1000 A.D.) that pharmacy was first delineated as a separate profession.

In America the pharmacist has always served as a necessary adjunct to the nation's physicians. Prior to the industrial revolution he personally compounded and prepared a large proportion of the remedies used in the practice of medicine. With the growth of pharmaceutical manufacturing, the technical work of compounding has been markedly reduced in the practice of the community pharmacist, although pharmacists continue to perform this vital function when necessary.

Today, nearly everyone is familiar with the pharmacist's major professional task—that of compounding and dispensing medications for individual patients. Not everyone is aware, however, of the knowledge and responsibility involved in performing this deceptively simple task. With the increasing number and sophistication of medicinal agents now available to combat disease, it has become even more important to have a highly trained health professional responsible for the safe and effective use of these products. The pharmacist is such a person.

There are presently about 130,000 pharmacists in the United States. About 100,000 practice in community settings, another

10,000 work in hospitals, and there are perhaps 10,000 in academic or industrial settings. About 10,000 pharmacists are either retired or professionally inactive. There is presently a great demand for pharmacists, since prescription volume has been increasing steadily at a rate of 10% a year for the last five or six years. This rate of increase should continue for some years to come, especially with the advent of government-supported health programs such as Medicare that have expanded the market for drugs and will no doubt eventually provide for outpatient prescription services as well as drugs for inpatients.

COMMUNITY PHARMACISTS AND PRESCRIPTION DRUGS

Most of today's pharmacists are employed in community or neighborhood pharmacies. They come into contact with literally hundreds of patients each week and dispense over one billion prescriptions a year. Each of those prescriptions represents an explicit order for a specific kind of drug for an individual patient. It is the responsibility of the pharmacist to determine whether the prescription includes the correct dosage, whether it will be compatible with other medications that the patient may be taking, and whether the directions for use are clear and complete. After selecting or preparing the proper drug and dosage form, the pharmacist must be sure that the medication is packaged in the right container and that the patient understands how to use it. For complete pharmaceutical service this usually requires a face-to-face discussion of the medication with the individual patient.

Obviously even the best of our modern drugs will be of no value if taken improperly or not at all. For example, many people think that a liquid antibiotic preparation for a baby's earache should be dripped directly into the ear rather than given orally. Some medications cause a patient's urine to change color, and unless he is told to expect this, a frantic call to the physician may result. A number of widely prescribed antibiotics are not absorbed properly if they are taken with milk. Since these products are often prescribed for children, a parent may give the child the capsule with a glass of milk, thus reducing the effectiveness of the therapy.

The pharmacist must also be alert to the possibility of drug interactions. With today's sophisticated drug therapy, it is not uncommon for a patient to be taking several drugs simultaneously, and some of these may interact with each other to the detriment of his health. Many patients today are under the care of several different physicians, and consequently a patient may receive prescriptions for the same drug from each. This is frequently the case with tranquilizers, since they are prescribed commonly by different kinds of specialists in medicine. Thus it is sometimes possible for a patient to be taking double or even triple the appropriate dosage of a particular drug, and this can sometimes result in dangerous overdoses. This type of problem is difficult to detect unless accurate drug histories of individual patients are kept. Many modern pharmacists are incorporating such patient prescription records into their practice. When a new patient comes to the pharmacist, he is asked to complete a patient record card, indicating any drug allergies or other problems that he may have. Other drugs that the patient may be taking are also recorded, so that every time a prescription is dispensed at that particular pharmacy, the patient's record card can be checked to see whether there are any possibilities of drug interactions or overdoses. The biggest drawback of this system is that the patient must have all of his prescriptions dispensed at one pharmacy if all drugs are to be noted on the record card. Pharmacists are now experimenting with filing patient prescription records from many pharmacies in a computer in an effort to overcome this problem. Any cooperating pharmacy could then draw needed information from the computer file through a simple telephone call.

OTHER FUNCTIONS OF COMMUNITY PHARMACISTS

As you can see, the pharmacist is in a strategic position to offer substantial professional services to the patient in connection with prescription drugs. However, this is by no means the only area in which he can make a contribution. The corner pharmacy is the largest source of self-medication products in the country, and the pharmacist is readily available to offer advice and counsel on the use of such agents. American families practice self-medication on a rather large basis; in fact, the typical family spends more than $35 each year on nonprescription drugs. Although the pharmacist is not trained to diagnose and prescribe drugs for medical problems, he is qualified to make comparative judgments on the quality and effectiveness of the drugs that he dispenses, and he is called upon to do this quite frequently in his everyday practice. Pharmacists also provide professional services by stocking and distributing surgical appliances and prescription accessories.

Some community pharmacists have expanded their professional services by acting as consultants to nursing homes and extended care facilities. Such facilities are usually not able to employ a full-time pharmacist and rely upon the neighborhood pharmacist to meet their pharmaceutical needs.

HOSPITAL PHARMACIES

Another major area of employment for practicing pharmacists is the hospital. In contrast to his colleague in the community, the hospital pharmacist is generally most concerned with serving the needs of inpatients at his institution, although some outpatient dispensing may be offered. In the hospital setting the pharmacist may also be responsible for such tasks as bulk compounding, the development and implementation of intravenous admixture programs, and the control of drug use within the institution. (See Fig. 8.) The hospital pharmacy often serves as a drug information center for

Fig. 8. A hospital pharmacist and physician discuss the choice of a patient's prescription drug.

the hospital and, in some instances, for the entire community. Here pharmacists, generally those who have some graduate training, analyze and compile information about drug products, including new drugs that may be available only for investigational use within the hospital.

Pharmacists in the hospital setting often come into contact with members of other health professions. For example, they may work in continuing education programs with physicians and other health workers. They may interact with the nursing staff in monitoring the drug therapy of inpatients and in attempting to minimize medication errors. They work with the medical dietitian, paying particular attention to food-drug interactions that may affect the well-being of the patient. For example, some foods may completely inactivate certain types of drugs, as in the case of the antibiotic-milk combination mentioned previously. In other cases, certain drug-food combinations may produce severe reactions in some patients.

Pharmacists may also be called upon to consult in poisoning cases, and the poison prevention centers in many hospitals are staffed by pharmacists. Drug therapy can sometimes change the normal values to be expected from certain laboratory diagnostic procedures, and therefore pharmacists and medical technologists often work closely together. Thus it is apparent that the pharmacist contributes to the well-being of the patient in the hospital in many ways beyond the mere compounding and dispensing of pharmaceuticals.

OTHER CAREER OPPORTUNITIES

Although community and hospital practices employ the largest number of pharmacy graduates, opportunities exist for pharmacists in a variety of other settings. The armed forces need pharmacists for military service, and the United States Public Health Service has opportunities in Indian health programs and federal hospitals. Pharmacists engage in health planning and administration through various federal and state agencies such as the Food and Drug Administration and state boards of pharmacy. Positions are available in the drug industry for pharmacists interested in laboratory work, drug development, and sales. Advanced degrees are generally required for research positions in industry or for teaching positions in the nation's seventy-six accredited colleges of pharmacy. It is clear that the unique training of the pharmacist provides for great flexibility in career choice upon graduation.

STARTING SALARIES

The pharmacy graduate of today commands perhaps the highest starting salary of any bachelor's degree graduate in the country. Positions in community pharmacy are financially rewarding, and especially attractive salaries are available in larger cities. Hospital salaries are somewhat lower, as are those paid for positions in government and industry. Pharmacists with advanced degrees may draw larger salaries.

WOMEN IN PHARMACY

The profession of pharmacy has become increasingly attractive to women, who comprise about 25% of the students in training today. Good salaries, flexible hours, and pleasant working conditions will probably continue to attract more women to the field.

EDUCATIONAL AND PRACTICAL REQUIREMENTS

The professional program in pharmacy is five years in length, and graduates earn the degree of Bachelor of Science in Pharmacy. The first two years consist of study in the basic sciences. These include general and organic chemistry, biology, anatomy, and physiology, physics, and mathematics. These requirements can often be met at community colleges or branch campuses of universities. The last three years must be spent in a college of pharmacy. Areas of study include pharmacognosy (the study of drugs of plant or animal origin), medicinal chemistry (the study of drugs of synthetic origin and the relation of the chemical structure of drug products to their action on the body), pharmacology (the study of the action of drug products on living systems), pharmaceutics (the study of the effect of dosage forms on drug activity), the social and administrative sciences (studies of the social, psychological, public health, and administrative aspects of the practice of pharmacy), and the clinical or professional practice area (the integration of material from the basic sciences and its applications to the practice of pharmacy).

After graduation from an accredited college of pharmacy, the aspiring pharmacist must take a licensing examination administered by the state board of pharmacy. This examination usually requires three days and includes theoretical examinations concerning the separate disciplines of the curriculum plus a practical examination. Most states require the completion of one year of internship in a pharmacy before the board examination may be taken. After successfully passing the examination, the candidate becomes licensed to practice pharmacy. There is reciprocity concerning licensure in some states. In others, the candidate must be reexamined.

ADVANCED EDUCATION PROGRAMS

Students who wish to pursue graduate studies in pharmacy may choose either professionally oriented or research oriented programs. Professional graduate degrees include the Doctor of Pharmacy and the master's degree in hospital pharmacy; both require two to three years of additional study, mainly in clinical areas. Some programs include residencies that offer practical experience in hospitals. Graduates of these programs assume positions of great responsibility in professional settings.

Research degrees at the master's and the doctor's levels are offered in each of the pharmaceutical sciences. Doctoral programs require three to five years of additional study and include a dissertation. They prepare graduates for research positions in industry or for academic positions.

SUMMARY

As this brief overview has shown, there is a distinct need for the services of properly educated pharmacists in a variety of positions. Pharmacists in all areas of practice and in every geographical location all share the primary responsibility of contributing to the safe and effective use of drugs by all who need them.

BIBLIOGRAPHY

Deno, R. A., Rowe, T. D., and Brodie, D. C.: The profession of pharmacy, Philadelphia, 1966, J. B. Lippincott Co.

Gable, F. B.: Opportunities in pharmacy careers, New York, 1964, Universal Publishing & Distributing Corp.

Sonnedecker, G. L.: Kremers and Urdang's history of pharmacy, ed. 3, Philadelphia, 1963, J. B. Lippincott Co.

PROFESSIONAL ORGANIZATION WHERE FURTHER INFORMATION CAN BE OBTAINED:

American Pharmaceutical Association
2215 Constitution Avenue, N.W.
Washington, D. C. 20037

Chapter 8

PHYSICAL THERAPY

Gladys G. Woods

Physical therapy is a challenging, stimulating, and continuously expanding health profession that offers a rewarding career for individuals who desire to work directly with people and who are interested in scientific and medical areas.

The physical therapist's functions involve the evaluation and treatment of a patient's physical abilities and disabilities. Patients of all ages are treated in an effort to improve their general health. These treatment programs may consist of teaching a patient to walk, to use an artificial limb, to improve his strength and coordination, or to alleviate pain through the use of various forms of heat, cold, ultrasound, or massage. The programs utilized are formulated from a knowledge of each patient's condition and the factors influencing it.

HISTORICAL DEVELOPMENTS

The first organized efforts to develop the profession of physical therapy in the United States were initiated during World War I. At that time a group of women who were practicing physical therapy formed the nucleus of the profession and were called "reconstruction aides." The first organized physical therapy department was established by the United States Army at the Walter Reed Army Hospital in Washington, D. C., and this department provided the impetus for further growth of the profession.

After the war ended, these women continued to perform their skills as civilians, and in 1921 the American Women's Therapeutic Association was formed. In 1922 the name was changed to the American Physiotherapy Association. This name stood until 1948, when it became the American Physical Therapy Association (APTA). This is now the official title of the organization.

The fifty-six chapters of the APTA, located throughout the United States, offer opportunities for professional growth to members. Each year a national conference offers physical therapists the opportunity to meet, share ideas, and advance their education. Members of the national organization consult with state and federal agencies, legislators, and other health organizations to support legislation that will provide funds for the operation of schools, faculty salaries, traineeships for students, and services to patients.

CONTRIBUTION TO HEALTH CARE

Physical therapists treat people of all ages and provide treatment procedures beneficial to a wide variety of disabilities. They make use of physical agents such as light, heat, cold, water, sound waves, and electricity, and they are skilled in the techniques of massage, therapeutic exercise, tests and measurements, and administrative procedures. (See Figs. 9 and 10.) Some of the common disabilities that confront the therapist include fractures, amputations, burns, strokes, arthritis, and congenital or traumatic spinal cord injuries.

Physical therapists are active participants in patient conferences, staff meetings, ward rounds, and clinics. They are responsible for sharing their professional knowledge of patients with all other members of the health team, and they in turn must know what other disciplines recommend. Physical therapists must cooperate with the other health team members in scheduling patients for treatment, writing comprehensive and periodic progress notes, submitting departmental reports on budget, and recording the number of patients treated, the number of visits by the patient to the

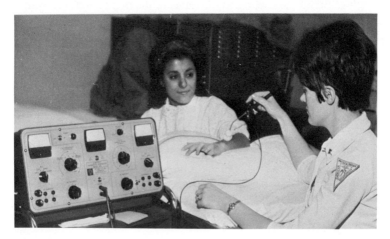

Fig. 9. The physical therapist uses electrical stimulation both for evaluation and muscle reeducation.

department, and the specific treatment administered. They must at all times be concerned with the patient's safety as well as with their own and that of the staff members in their department.

The following case study serves to illustrate some of the treatment procedures that are the responsibility of the physical therapist.

R. S., 25 years of age, had a right midthigh amputation. A referral for treatment was sent by his physician to the physical therapy department of a large hospital ten days after the surgery. The physical therapist in the department was instructed to evaluate the patient and establish postamputation training.

Mrs. X., the physical therapist, visited R. S. in his room. After she introduced herself, she evaluated the stump of his right thigh for shape and skin condition and gave instructions for its hygienic care. R. S. was taught the proper technique of wrapping it with an Ace bandage to reduce swelling and to obtain proper shape for desirable prosthetic fitting. The therapist also evaluated the range of motion and the strength of the patient's right hip. He was

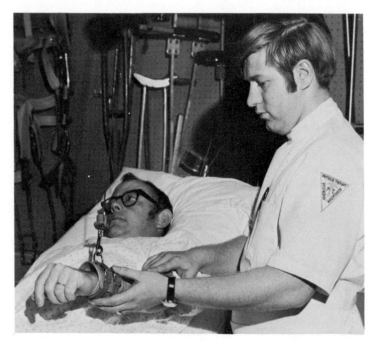

Fig. 10. Developing strength, coordination, and endurance of major muscle groups is part of rehabilitation.

measured for crutches and they were ordered. He was scheduled for further physical therapy activity later that day.

During his first session in the physical therapy department, R. S. began preliminary training for crutch ambulation by walking in the parallel bars and started exercises designed to strengthen his shoulders, arms, left leg, right stump, and hip. A balance routine and ambulation on a level surface with crutches were initiated, and he began to practice standing and sitting techniques. After reexamining the patient's wrapped stump, Mrs. X. outlined the evaluation and rehabilitation program for department and hospital chart records.

During the second week, Mrs. X. worked with R. S. twice a day in the physical therapy department. He progressed through resistive exercises involving all extremities and practiced stair climbing and walking with his crutches over rough ground, curbs, and similar surfaces. At the same time he was receiving psychological, vocational, and social counseling and reinforcement to aid him in adjusting to his disability.

Prior to his discharge the patient was evaluated in the prosthetic clinic by physicians and the physical therapist to determine the type of prosthesis best suited for him.

At the end of the second week, R. S. was discharged by his physician and the type of prosthesis determined by the evaluation was ordered. He returned as an outpatient a month later and began a series of five daily training sessions in the use of his artificial limb. This training involved balance, gait, and care of the prosthesis. R. S. was scheduled to be rechecked in two months, with the option of returning earlier if any problems should arise.

Eventually his skills would be evaluated in terms of vocational opportunities, and the final training sessions would be directed toward helping R. S. prepare for employment.

EDUCATIONAL REQUIREMENTS

To become a qualified physical therapist, one must have successfully completed an approved course of study in physical therapy at an accredited college or university. Accreditation of the physical therapy program is provided by the Council on Medical Education of the AMA in conjunction with the APTA. An academic program offering a bachelor's degree requires four years of college-level work. The first two years are usually preprofessional and include courses in English, mathematics, the natural and social sciences, and the humanities. The last two years include advanced science courses, professional physical therapy courses, clinical education, and medical information.

Sixteen of the fifty-six accredited schools of physical therapy offer certificate programs to the student who holds a baccalaureate degree. Successful completion of basic courses in the natural sciences is necessary for admission into these programs, and twelve to sixteen months are usually required to complete the professional courses and clinical education.

Successful completion of the APTA written examination provided by the Professional Examination Service (PES) of the American Public Health Association is accepted as one of the qualifications for licensure in forty-six states. Other requirements include payment of dues and fees, a good moral character, and other such qualifications as each state may establish. A reciprocal agreement among most states permits the practitioner licensed in one state to apply for licensure in another without reexamination.

It is possible for students to apply for admission to a graduate program leading to a master's degree either in physical therapy or in a related field such as anatomy, psychology, or education.

PROFESSIONAL QUALITIES

Physical therapists are professionals who serve people by working with them to help them overcome physical limitations. Physical therapists should therefore enjoy working with people and should be sensitive to the physical, psychological, and sociological needs of others. In order to be effective, physical therapists must be able to adjust to various patient personalities and disabilities while maintaining emotional self-control. During unusual or emergency situations, therapists must demonstrate sound judgment, emotional stability, and common sense. Reliability, attention to detail, and a high degree of motivation, imagination, and initiative are all attributes that enhance the physical therapist's effectiveness.

Both men and women can function competently as physical therapists. Age and stature are not limiting factors so long as the individual is in general good physical condition and has the strength and endurance necessary for continuous work performance.

Salary depends on many variables, including the size, type, and location of the facility, professional experience, and amount of responsibility assumed by the physical therapist. Salaries range from $8,000 to $11,000 annually for newly graduated physical therapists. In general, they compare favorably with salaries paid to other health professionals with equivalent amounts of training.

SUPPORTIVE PERSONNEL

The two types of supportive personnel recognized by the APTA are the physical therapy assistant and the physical therapy aide.

The assistant's educational requirements may be met in a two-year associate degree program in a community or junior college. This program consists of preprofessional and professional courses, some of which may be acceptable for transfer credit toward a degree in physical therapy. Following completion of an approved curriculum, the assistant is prepared to perform administrative procedures, to treat patients by the use of specific techniques, and to help with supportive operational duties under the supervision of a qualified physical therapist. He is not trained to perform evaluative procedures, prepare treatment plans, or to assume responsibility for total administration within the department.

The physical therapy aide's training program consists of on-the-job training and in-service education within an established physical therapy department under the supervision of a qualified physical therapist. No degree, certificate, or other formal recognition is given upon completion of this program. The aide may function only under constant supervision of the professional physical therapist and he may be given responsibilities in the areas of department equipment maintenance, supply requisition, housekeeping, and specific patient-related activities.

EMPLOYMENT OPPORTUNITIES

The physical therapist is an important member of the health care team. The majority of physical therapists work in hospital physical therapy departments. They are also employed in various community agencies and programs such as the Arthritis Foundation, Easter Seal Societies for Crippled Children and Adults, and the National Elks Foundation (of the Benevolent Protective Order of Elk of the United States of America) as well as in state and federal public health services and programs for the mentally retarded. Physical therapists also serve in the armed forces. Salaries for positions in these areas range from $7,500 to $10,000 annually for the recent graduate who works under the supervision of an experienced therapist.

Physical therapists with greater clinical experience and knowledge may be employed as consultants to nursing homes, community health projects, and small rural hospitals. These therapists provide guidance for the development of physical therapy programs in these types of facilities through in-service education and training of personnel, and they participate in the treatment of the patient population.

Many therapists are self-employed and treat patients referred by physicians. They may treat patients in their offices on an outpatient basis, contract with various facilities such as nursing homes, or go into patients' homes. Men may participate in athletic training programs and may become qualified both as physical therapists and athletic trainers.

There are teaching opportunities for professionally qualified physical therapists either as full- or part-time university faculty members or as supervisors of student affiliates in clinical settings. Graduate education and clinical experience are required for academic advancement. The development of programs to train physical therapy assistants, the opening of new schools for educating physical therapists, and the continuing need for teaching personnel in the fifty-one existing schools have created a great demand for qualified faculty.

Part-time employment is also available because there are more demands for trained therapists than there are people to fill the positions. Physical therapists who became professionally inactive to marry and raise children are being encouraged to help meet the critical need even though they cannot work full time.

CURRENT STATISTICS

There are approximately 13,000 members of the APTA and approximately 20,000 qualified physical therapists in the United States. The profession loses about 20% of its members each year due to marriage, retirement, and other factors. As a result, there is a greater demand for therapists than can presently be met by new graduates. It is estimated that a 30% increase in the number of therapists would be required to provide adequate physical therapy service in the United States. Each year about 1,300 students are graduated from fifty-six approved schools.

With the advent of recent federally supported health programs, the role of the physical therapist has greatly expanded. These changes include allocation of greater responsibilities, increased collaboration with other disciplines, and the authority to make diagnoses formerly limited to physicians. The recognized value of the profession in restoring physical independence, in evaluating health care needs relating to various patient disabilities, and in providing consultative services to physicians, hospital administrators, and other similar health professionals has created support for programs to train greater numbers of physical therapists.

BIBLIOGRAPHY

Handbook for physical therapy teachers, Washington, D. C., 1967, American Physical Therapy Association.

Hospitals, "Guide Issue" (part II) **42:**entire issue, 1968.

Krumhansl, B.: Opportunities in physical therapy, New York, 1968, Universal Publishing & Distributing Corp., pp. 109-112.

Licht, E.: Therapeutic exercise, Baltimore, 1965, Waverly Press, Inc.

Pattison, H.: The handicapped and their rehabilitation, Springfield, Ill., 1957, Charles C Thomas, Publisher.

Rusk, H.: Rehabilitation medicine, ed. 3, St. Louis, 1971, The C. V. Mosby Co.

PROFESSIONAL ORGANIZATION WHERE FURTHER INFORMATION CAN BE OBTAINED:

American Physical Therapy Association
1156 15th Street, N.W.
Washington, D. C. 20005

Chapter 9

DENTAL HYGIENE

Nancy M. Reynolds

Dental hygiene is an auxiliary profession of dentistry and is one of the allied health professions. Its function, as defined by the American Dental Association (ADA), is to assist the members of the dental profession in providing oral health care to the public.

Dental hygiene is practiced by dental hygienists—sometimes called oral hygienists. They are licensed, professional oral health educators and clinical operators who, as auxiliaries to the dentist, use scientific methods in the control and prevention of oral disease, helping individuals and groups to develop and maintain optimum oral health. A dental hygienist's work involves preventive dentistry, which includes dental health education (the teaching of the methods of prevention to individual patients or to groups of individuals) and those clinical procedures (including oral prophylaxis) that are delegated by the dental profession.

BACKGROUND

Dental hygiene is a new profession when compared to dentistry, medicine, and nursing. Dr. Alfred C. Fones, a dentist, opened the first school for dental hygienists in 1913 in Bridgeport, Connecticut. He was convinced that general health could be improved by good oral health, and his main purpose in educating dental hygienists was to prepare them to work in the public schools in Bridgeport. In the schools, dental hygienists are oral health educators, teaching children proper oral hygiene habits to help them reduce dental decay and improve their oral health.

EDUCATIONAL PROGRAMS

Between 1957 and 1970 the number of accredited dental hygiene programs in the United States increased from thirty-three to seventy, and many more programs are currently being developed. All dental hygiene programs must meet the standards established by the Council on Dental Education of the American Dental Association, which is comprised of representatives from the American

Dental Hygienists' Association and the ADA. Admission requirements include the completion of a minimum of two academic years of college-level study at an accredited university, college, or junior college. Basic biology is usually a requirement for admission. Chemistry and mathematics are not always required, but it is usually recommended that students study these subjects either in high school or college. High school mathematics or test performance at a level indicating a basic knowledge of mathematics is often required.

Most schools also require that prospective dental hygiene students take the aptitude test administered by the American Dental Hygienists' Association. The test results are considered in conjunction with the applicant's other qualifications.

Traditionally, dental hygiene curricula were associated with schools of dentistry, but in recent years dental hygiene programs have been offered in two-year schools as well as in four-year colleges and universities. Various options are available to the prospective dental hygienist. Two-year junior or community colleges award an associate degree to those who successfully complete the program. Four-year colleges and universities may either offer certificates designating as graduate dental hygienists those who successfully complete the two-year program, or they may award baccalaureate degrees to those who complete the degree requirements plus the requirements for the dental hygiene program. The baccalaureate programs may integrate the university's arts and sciences requirements with an increasing emphasis on dental hygiene courses in each of the succeeding years, or the dental hygiene program may be concentrated in two of the four years of enrollment. A few programs in the United States are offered jointly with a college of education. In this type of program, students are required to do practice teaching in both general and dental health in an elementary school. Upon successful completion of this program, the graduate receives a bachelor of science degree in education and a teaching certificate. The combined education-dental hygiene program offers preparation for the dental hygiene profession as well as teacher preparation for dental health programs in schools, in the general community, and in schools of dental hygiene.

Some universities offer programs for the graduate dental hygienist leading to a master's degree. These may concern dental hygiene, health education, public health, education, or basic science. Among the institutions currently offering such programs are The Ohio State University, Columbus; Columbia University, New York

City; the University of Michigan, Ann Arbor; the University of Iowa, Iowa City; the University of Missouri–Kansas City School of Dentistry; and the University of Washington, Seattle.

CURRICULUM

Basic science requirements in dental hygiene programs include anatomy, microbiology, and physiology. Specific courses in English, health education, nutrition, psychology, sociology, and speech are also required.

A dental hygiene curriculum also includes course work in anesthesia, chemistry, dental anatomy, dental materials, dental nursing techniques, general pathology, oral histology and pathology, oral hygiene and oral hygiene programs for schools, pharmacology, practice management, public health, and radiography. Clinical experience is an important part of the dental hygiene curriculum, and courses in oral prophylaxis provide this experience. (See Fig. 11.)

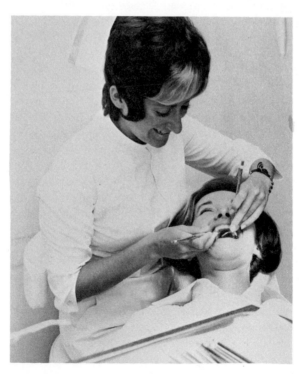

Fig. 11. Clinical application of dental hygiene procedures is an important part of the curriculum. A student performs an oral prophylaxis on a patient.

LICENSING

In order to be licensed to practice, most dental hygienists take the written examination administered by the National Dental Hygiene Board, which is recognized in forty-eight states, the District of Columbia, and the Virgin Islands. Those states and territories not using National Board results are Delaware, New Jersey, and Puerto Rico. In addition, most states require that the dental hygienist pass a practical examination.

FUNCTIONS OF THE DENTAL HYGIENIST AND CAREER OPPORTUNITIES

The dental hygienist is licensed to treat the patient in a private office or clinic by performing oral prophylaxis as well as other services for the patient. Dental hygienists may apply topical fluorides that make the surface of the tooth harder and less vulnerable to disease and may expose and develop radiographs of the oral structures. The hygienist also assists the dentist by recognizing and reporting abnormalities of the oral cavity. A most important part of the dental hygienist's work involves educating each individual to his own oral health needs and responsibilities in effectively preventing oral disease.

In many states, laws have been or are now being changed to permit an expansion of the duties of this important dental auxiliary. Additional functions may include polishing restorations (fillings), placing sedative restorations, and taking impressions for making models of the teeth. An effective dental hygienist frees the dentist to perform only those services that require his skill and competence.

Dental hygienists who are employed in schools work directly to meet the foremost goal of the profession—education of the public. They are largely responsible for planning and executing that portion of the curriculum that pertains to their special field and for actually performing dental hygiene services if such treatment is provided in the school.

There are opportunities for employment in government institutions and programs, in industrial health programs, in research, in hospitals, and in the United States Army Medical Corps where dental hygienists serve as commissioned officers. There are some positions available in foreign countries through the Peace Corps, on the hospital ship *Hope,* and with privately sponsored health care projects.

Although most dental hygienists are women, men are also welcome in the profession. Many male dental hygienists serve as health professionals in the armed services. Salaries paid to full-time dental hygienists vary considerably and depend upon geographical location and the size and nature of the employing institution or facility as well as upon the dental hygienist's training, experience, and professional responsibilities. In general, dental hygienists earn a beginning salary of $6,000 to $8,000 annually.

PERSONAL QUALIFICATIONS

Those who are interested in the profession of dental hygiene should exhibit traits of personality and character that are consistent with the responsibilities they will assume upon entering a health profession—responsibilities to the profession and to the public. Those who are unable or unwilling to give these responsibilities first priority in a professional situation should not enter the field of dental hygiene.

Successful dental hygienists are sympathetic to every human being and his needs, are meticulous about detail, and are perfectionists in every facet of practice but patient in those instances where perfection cannot be achieved. They regard the profession of dentistry with respect.

PROFESSIONAL ORGANIZATIONS

The professional organization for dental hygienists is the American Dental Hygienists' Association. Affiliated with this organization is a students' counterpart, the Junior American Dental Hygienists' Association. Students are encouraged to join and participate in this organization so that they may learn about the professional organization that governs and protects them. Student members as well as professionals receive the *Journal of the American Dental Hygienists' Association,* the official publication of the organization.

SIGMA PHI ALPHA

Sigma Phi Alpha is the national dental hygiene honor society. Senior dental hygiene students who are outstanding in scholarship, leadership, and professional attitude are candidates for election to the society. The number of students elected annually from each class may not exceed 10% of the total number of students in the graduating class.

BIBLIOGRAPHY

Wilkins, E. M., and McCullough, P. A.: Clinical practice of the dental hygienist, ed. 2, Philadelphia, 1964, Lea & Febiger.

PROFESSIONAL ORGANIZATION WHERE FURTHER INFORMATION CAN BE OBTAINED:

American Dental Hygienists' Association
211 East Chicago Avenue
Chicago, Illinois 60611

Chapter 10

DIETETICS

Burness G. Wenberg and Barbara K. Martin

Altering a person's nutritional status may affect his physical condition, performance, personality, disposition, appearance, and life-span. New discoveries are constantly being made in the fields of medicine and nutrition. New and better methods and procedures for preparing and serving food appear almost daily, and new food products on the market have become almost commonplace. As a result, the profession of dietetics continues to change, grow, and expand to serve people better.

The dietitian is committed to improving human nutrition, advancing the science of dietetics and nutrition, and promoting education in these and allied areas. Food is the tool that the dietitian uses in illustrating and promoting good nutrition. Professional dietitians work with persons of all ages in a variety of institutional and agency settings. (See Fig. 12.) Hospitals and health care facilities claim the greatest number of dietitians. They are also found in elementary, secondary, college, and university food services. Others may be employed in business and industry. Teaching at the college level and research in food and nutrition are additional careers for dietitians. For those persons interested in working with food and people, a variety of opportunities are available.

HOW DID THE PROFESSION DEVELOP?

Although the profession of dietetics is relatively young, its background reaches into antiquity. The Ebers papyrus, written a thousand years before Hippocrates, contained what may be the first recorded diet prescription. The famous French scientist Lavoisier made a revolutionary contribution to nutrition in 1794 by making laboratory determinations of the end results of digestive activities. For opening the door to scientific research in this field, he is accepted as the father of nutrition.

Continuing inquiry in this century has produced methods that make it possible to measure energy transformation in the body, to

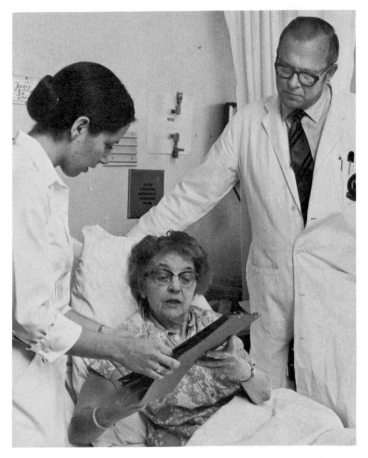

Fig. 12. Patients often work with the clinical dietitian and physician to plan the best dietary pattern to meet their nutritional requirements.

determine the exact nutritive values of food materials, and to determine the roles of proteins, minerals, vitamins, and other nutrients in the functioning of the body. Formerly the dietitian was associated with the feeding of sick persons and worked almost exclusively in hospitals. As the science of nutrition developed, the dietitian assumed the additional responsibility of applying research findings to the work of feeding groups of people.

The services of dietitians were in great demand during World War I, both in Europe with the armed forces and at home, where they faced the problem of feeding people in institutions despite the limitations imposed by food rationing and food shortages. Expressing a need to share their knowledge and seek better solutions to their problems, a small group of dietitians met in Cleveland, Ohio, in 1917 to organize the American Dietetic Association. The new organization's greatest impact may have resulted from its identification of educational requirements for curricula in dietetics and from its subsequent work with colleges, universities, and hospitals to implement these new standards.

Prior to 1917 there were a few "student dietitian" programs in hospitals. The applicants' qualifications ranged from a high school diploma to a college degree. By 1935 some sixty hospitals and institutions offered programs approved by the American Dietetic Association for the professional education of dietitians. Applicants to these programs were required to present a college degree, with successful completion of courses in foods, nutrition, and chemistry. As the number of dietitians as well as the quality of their training increased, both the profession and the professional organization gained in strength and stature. The professional dietitian achieved recognition as the person skilled in providing quality nutritional care to individuals and groups.

WHAT PARTICULAR QUALITIES ARE NEEDED?

Young men and women should consider careers in dietetics if they (1) find studying the biological and behavioral sciences stimulating, (2) are interested in the nutritional, sociological, and psychological effects of foods on people, (3) enjoy working directly with people, and (4) gain personal satisfaction from using their knowledge to benefit mankind. The ability to be creative and innovative in the preparation and service of food is especially valuable to prospective dietitians. These individuals are entering a highly respected and relevant profession—a profession whose major concern is the welfare of humanity.

WHAT IS THE EDUCATIONAL PREPARATION?

Those who want to become professionally qualified dietitians will find that a variety of pathways lead to their goal. All accredited programs, however, require a baccalaureate degree and undergraduate work that includes stated minimum academic requirements. In addition, one is required to successfully complete a component of professional dietetic education that has been approved by the American Dietetic Association. A variety of approved programs to prepare qualified dietitians are currently available. Some are coordinated clinical-didactic undergraduate programs, while others are postbaccalaureate dietetic internships or graduate programs. Although some are specialized dietetic programs, the majority are more general. As different programs appeal to different students, they will be described separately.

High school

Preparation for a career in dietetics should begin in high school. College preparatory courses in chemistry, mathematics, biology, and the social sciences are highly recommended.

Undergraduate coordinated programs

Coordinated programs for undergraduates were first offered at The Ohio State University in the 1960s, and now an increasing number of colleges and universities throughout the United States are either offering or planning to offer such a curriculum. The total professional education is incorporated in course work required for the baccalaureate degree. Clinical experience is usually introduced in the junior year and increases in depth and scope with each succeeding term. Those who successfully complete the curriculum are recommended for membership in the American Dietetic Association.

Some programs are described as focusing on general dietetics, while others have a food management or clinical dietetics emphasis. Only those colleges and universities that have adequate clinical facilities can offer this more specialized type of program, which has the advantage of orienting students to the typical clinical setting for the practice of dietetics early in their educational experience.

College preparation for the dietetic internship

A great many colleges and universities offer a major in dietetics, foods and nutrition, the nutritional sciences, or food management. The majority of these curricula are offered in departments of home economics, but in some instances these courses will be found in other academic departments. The basic academic requirements are met with such a major. Specific course requirements include nutrition, foods, chemistry, physiology, and bacteriology. Depending on the interest of the student or the requirements of the curriculum, additional courses will emphasize general dietetics, food management, or nutritional care and research.

Successful completion of the curriculum and the awarding of the baccalaureate degree qualify the graduate to apply for either a dietetic internship, graduate study in dietetics, or both.

Dietetic internships

Dietetic internships provide an opportunity for the dietetic intern to practice in depth the principles of nutritional care and food management learned in college. Under the guidance of an experienced staff and faculty, the dietetic intern adds to his basic knowledge and develops his own professional behavioral style. The dietetic internship has been traditionally viewed as the "fifth year," but since early 1970, there have been many innovations in both existing and developing dietetic internships. Programs are now offered that vary in length from six to eight, nine, ten, twelve, fifteen, and eighteen months. Approved dietetic internships are offered in a variety of institutions: hospitals, nutrition clinics, industrial food services, school food services, state institutions, and colleges and universities. Basically, nutritional care in a hospital or an outpatient clinic and food management in a variety of food service settings are emphasized. Successful completion of a dietetic internship qualifies the graduate for membership in the American Dietetic Association.

Additional pathways

One can qualify for membership in the American Dietetic Association by earning a graduate degree and accumulating successful work experience. Recipients of a master's degree in foods, nutrition, or public health nutrition must have twelve months of acceptable work experience under the supervision of a professionally qualified dietitian. The recipient of a doctoral degree in any of these areas of specialization is immediately eligible for membership. Effective in July 1971, candidates who have met the minimum academic requirements and have a baccalaureate degree can apply for participation in a preplanned two-year professional work program under the supervision of a professionally qualified dietitian. Those who obtain prior approval of the plan and complete it successfully are qualified for membership. Further information regarding any of these approved educational programs is available from the American Dietetic Association.

WHO IS THE REGISTERED DIETITIAN?

The registered dietitian is responsible for planning, directing, and evaluating food management and nutritional care services and for educational and research programs in the field of dietetics. A registered dietitian is a member of the American Dietetic Association who successfully completes a required number of continuing education hours every five years. The concept of professional registration was adopted by the members of the Association in 1969, and registration is voluntary for members. Each member is free to participate or to abstain, and continuing membership in the Association remains entirely unaffected by participation or nonparticipation in the plan. An examination is required of those applying for registration, and to remain registered, the dietitian must complete a total of seventy-five clock hours of continuing education over each five-year period, be a member of the Association, and pay the annual registration fee. Registration was adopted with the goal of maintaining and enhancing the standards of the profession and the individual practitioner.

WHERE DO DIETITIANS WORK?

There are many areas of service available to the dietitian. Many choose to work in hospitals or clinics, while some prefer the atmosphere of nursing homes or extended care facilities. Others find research, community health services, food management, or teaching especially rewarding. Dietitians may find that they are the only member of their profession employed in a given setting, or they may be a member of a dietetic staff that ranges in size from two to as many as the twenty-five or thirty professionals found in large teaching hospitals.

Clinical dietitians employed in hospitals or extended care facilities work closely with physicians and other health care personnel in selecting appropriate diets and in providing dietary care. Those working in a nutrition clinic or with groups involved in community health projects will be associated with physicians, social workers, and public health nurses. They may participate in individual counseling and group education. The clinical dietitian may find it helpful or even necessary to visit some people in their homes to assist them with the wise purchasing, storage, and preparation of foods.

What specifically might the clinical dietitian's job be? Miss Jones is employed by the Nutrition Services Department of a large medical center. She is one of a staff of eight dietitians and is responsible to Miss Webster, the head dietitian of the Service. Miss Jones is assigned to a ninety-patient medical unit, and she works with all of the health professionals on that unit. Her working day usually runs from 7:30 A.M. to 4:30 P.M. She begins her day by checking with the dietetic technician on new admissions, diet changes, and planned discharges of patients. Today Miss Jones must meet with three patients who are going home by 10:00 A.M.

She promised to see them before they left in case they had any additional questions about the low-salt diets they are to follow at home. There are also ten new patients to be seen. Miss Jones' task is to assess their need for nutrition counseling and make plans for any further dietary counseling. Between 9:00 and 11:00 A.M. she works with those patients in need of dietary counseling.

As this is Tuesday, it is the day of the chief of staff's weekly luncheon conference with medical students, interns, and residents. Miss Jones participates in these conferences of patient presentations and contributes her knowledge to the identification and solution of their nutritional problems. From 2:00 to 3:00 P.M. she participates in daily class activities that the unit presents for all of the patients with diabetes. Today Miss Jones has the class on diet. As soon as she returns from class, the head nurse calls her to report difficulty with the 2:30 P.M. tube feeding for one of the patients. Miss Jones checks immediately and discovers that the recipe she developed had not been followed. To resolve the problem, Miss Jones supervises its preparation so she may be certain that the patient receives what he should and that the food service worker understands how to follow the new recipe. That was Tuesday! Wednesday will bring some of the same activities, but there will be a whole new set of challenges as well.

The administrative or food management dietitian is responsible for planning the menu, ordering the required food, and organizing and supervising the food service workers who prepare and serve food to the clientele. The clientele may be children in school lunch programs, students who participate in college and university food service programs, employees in industrial cafeterias, customers in commercial cafeterias, or patients in hospitals or extended care facilities. In fact, administrative dietitians can be involved wherever food is served to groups of people.

Let us look at the typical day of a dietitian in a school lunch program to gain a better understanding of the work of a food management dietitian. Miss Smith is the only dietitian employed in the new school district. There are five elementary schools and a junior and a senior high school in the district. The total enrollment is 2,000 students. The kitchen is located in the senior high school, and food prepared there is transported by truck to the other schools. Miss Smith has a staff of three dietetic technicians and twelve food service workers. When she arrives at 8:00 A.M., Miss Smith checks with the dietetic technicians to ensure that the assigned workers are on duty and that all the food needed for the day is available. Her calendar for today includes a meeting with one of the fifth grade classes at 10:00 A.M. to assist the teacher in presenting a nutrition unit. Miss Smith must also check on a complaint that food is cold when it arrives at the junior high school at 11:30 A.M. She meets at 1:30 P.M. with one of the elementary school PTAs to finalize plans for a spaghetti supper and must attend the superintendent's meeting with all the school district's principals at 3:00 P.M. to discuss the defeat of the operating tax levy at the previous day's election. Today is Thursday, and therefore the orders for all of next week's deliveries of meat and fresh vegetables and fruit must be placed. As you can see, this food management dietitian must be able to work with people, must enjoy working with food, and must be ready to seek solutions to a variety of problems.

These are just two examples of the dietitian's world of work. Nutrition research, college teaching, and many other opportunities are available to the qualified dietitian.

WHAT IS THE NEED FOR DIETITIANS?

Dietitians are in great demand today, and this demand will continue to increase for many years to come. Presently there are 20,000 members of the American Dietetic Association, approximately 300 of whom are men. The percentage of men entering the field is increasing each year.

It is estimated that by 1980, 56,000 qualified dietitians will be needed. In order to satisfy this need, approximately 5,000 persons should be entering the field each year through 1980, but in fact, fewer than 1,000 join the profession each year.

Because the supply is not meeting the demand, job opportunities available to those entering the field are many and varied. Salaries continue to increase, and fringe benefits become more attractive. The American Dietetic Association has recommended a minimum annual salary of $8,000 for the dietitian I as of 1971. The dietitian I is defined as a member of the Association who has completed all educational requirements but has acquired no professional work experience. The dietitian II is defined as a member of the Association who has met the requirements for registered dietitian. The recommended minimum annual salary for the beginning registered dietitian is $9,000.

WHO ARE THE SUPPORTING PROFESSIONALS?

Departments of dietetics in most large institutions such as hospitals, extended care facilities, and cafeterias will employ people who are qualified to assist the dietitian in specific areas of food management and nutritional care service.

Dietetic technicians

Dietetic technicians are personnel skilled in food management or nutritional care who have successfully completed an associate degree program for dietetic technicians that meets the standards of the American Dietetic Association. They work under the supervision of a dietitian or an administrator and a consulting dietitian. Their educational background prepares them to assist in providing and assessing food management or nutritional care services. They are qualified to assist the dietitian in food preparation, food service, or patient nutritional care in health care facilities, educational institutions, or industry. There are currently about 150 approved programs for dietetic technicians in two-year colleges throughout the United States. It is estimated that there are 6,000 employed dietetic technicians.

Dietetic assistants

Dietetic assistants have a high school diploma or the equivalent and have successfully completed a course in food service management or nutritional care that meets the standards established by the American Dietetic Association. They work under the close supervision of the dietetic technician, dietitian, or consulting dietitian. Their work in food management or nutritional care services might include ordering food, maintaining records, planning and assigning the duties of dietetic or food service workers, or assisting patients in menu selection. Like the dietetic technician, dietetic assistants may be employed in food service departments of health care facilities, educational institutions, or industry. There are many avenues by which a person may become a dietetic assistant. The required curriculum may be available in vocational high school programs, adult education programs, technical institutes, or through a correspondence course offered in cooperation with a food service department.

Both of these supporting professionals play an important role in the dietetic or food service department. Their major objective is to contribute to the nutritional welfare of the patient or client. Their duties may vary somewhat, depending on the size and type of institution for which they work, but they are always interesting and rewarding.

SUMMARY

Dietetics is one of the well-established health professions that is concerned with both sick and well persons. Food is the tool the dietitian uses to promote nutrition by assisting in the maintenance of good health and in the prevention and treatment of disease. Prospective dietetic students may choose from a variety of educational programs and, depending on their interests and abilities, may select one of a number of available areas for an in-depth study of dietetics. As food—nutritious food—is essential to life, there will always be a need for dietitians.

BIBLIOGRAPHY

Allied health manpower, 1950-80, Publication No. 263, Sec. 21, Washington, D. C., 1970, Department of Health, Education, and Welfare, United States Public Health Service.

Dietetics as a profession, Chicago, 1966, The American Dietetic Association.

Kinsinger, R. E., editor: Health technicians, Chicago, 1970, J. G. Ferguson Publishing Co.

Position paper on recommended salaries and employment practices for members of the American Dietetic Association, J. Amer. Diet. Ass. **58**:41, 1971.

Your future as a dietitian, New York, 1964, Richards Rosen Press, Inc.

PROFESSIONAL ORGANIZATION WHERE ADDITIONAL INFORMATION CAN BE OBTAINED:

American Dietetic Association
620 North Michigan Avenue
Chicago, Illinois 60611

Chapter 11

INHALATION THERAPY

O. Theodore Haaland

SCIENTIFIC HISTORY

Concern with the mystery of "breath as life" is apparent early in man's history, whereas the development of a cadre of health professionals dedicated to the amelioration of respiratory ills is a quite recent occurrence. The tale of the biblical prophet Elijah's use of apparent mouth-to-mouth resuscitation is fairly well known, as are the experiments of Aristotle in the fourth century B.C. in which small animals were observed to die when placed in airtight boxes. The fifteenth century anatomist Andreas Vesalius maintained heart pulsations and life in an animal by blowing into a hollow reed he inserted in its trachea. The experimental efforts of the seventeenth century English chemists, notably Robert Boyle and Robert Hooke, greatly enhanced scientific interest in mammalian respiration and expanded man's knowledge of the physical nature and activity of gases. Toward the latter part of the eighteenth century, just prior to the American Revolution, "dephlogisticated air"[1] (named in accordance with the erroneous hypotheses then current) was produced in the laboratory of Joseph Priestley as well as by the Swedish chemist Scheele. Priestley's notes regarding experiments with this gas—shortly to be named oxygen by the brilliant Frenchman Antoine Lavoisier—are piquant:

> My reader will not wonder that, having ascertained the superior goodness of dephlogisticated air by mice living in it, and the other tests mentioned above, I should have the curiosity to taste it myself . . . I have gratified that curiosity by breathing it, drawing it through a glass syphon, and by this means I reduced a large jar full of it to the standard of common air, but I fancied that

[1]George Ernst Stahl, professor of physiology at Halle, Germany, propounded an erroneous theory in which a substance called phlogiston was thought to be given off during combustion. Stahl's hypothesis bedeviled chemistry for decades, and Priestly never forsook his adherence to it, having failed to draw correct conclusions from his numerous gas experiments.

my breath felt peculiarly light and easy for some time afterwards. Who can tell but that in time this pure air may become a fashionable article in luxury. Hitherto, only two mice and myself have had the privilege of breathing it.[2]

The discovery of oxygen and other medical gases set the stage for the first serious (and some not-so-serious) attempts at providing a beneficient artificial atmosphere for human inhalation. Thomas Beddoes, an English physician, held that a wide variety of disorders could be relieved by the breathing of manufactured airs of varying gas content, and in 1798 he established the Pneumatic Institute to provide such treatments. By the mid-nineteenth century, breathing both oxygen and nitrous oxide had become something akin to a parlor sport. One itinerant organizer of these "laughing gas frolics" along the Eastern seaboard of the United States was Samuel Colt, who controlled his own levity sufficiently to develop the firearm that bears his name.

Ventilatory therapeutics was established on a sound basis near the beginning of the twentieth century. World Wars I and II helped to accelerate interest in developing methods of respiratory augmentation, giving rise to the use of oxygen through a variety of techniques to combat the effects of gas poisoning in World War I and to the development during World War II of high-altitude oxygen masks and demand-breathing valves—the precursors of present clinical ventilators.

PROFESSIONAL HISTORY

At this point the development of inhalation therapy as an allied health profession will be outlined. A regularly scheduled series of lectures was begun in the Chicago area in the mid-1940s that dealt with correct respiratory therapeutic practice, and this groundwork culminated in the formation of the Inhalation Therapy Association. In 1970 the Committee on Public Health Relations of the New York Academy of Medicine published standards for inhalation therapy. In 1955 the Inhalation Therapy Association, under the sponsorship of the American College of Chest Physicians (ACCP) and the American Society of Anesthesiologists (ASA), became the American Association of Inhalation Therapists. In 1966 this was changed to the American Association for Inhalation Therapy (AAIT), which is the organization's current official title.

[2]Priestley, J.: Experiments and observations on different kinds of air, London, 1775, J. Johnson, vol. 2, sec. 5, p. 104.

The profession has continued to develop in cooperation with other closely related professional organizations. The American Registry of Inhalation Therapists (ARIT), founded in Illinois in 1960, is an organization committed to achieving the highest standards of technical practice through education and the development of examination procedures. In 1962 the first edition of *Essentials for an Approved School of Inhalation Therapy* was published under the aegis of the Council on Medical Education of the AMA. A revised edition was published in 1967.

From a struggling organization only fifteen years ago but with taproots extending back centuries, inhalation therapy has become a vigorous allied health profession of approximately 10,000 practitioners, more than 1,400 of whom are registered in their field. The

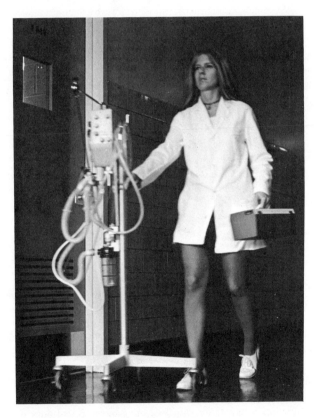

Fig. 13. Prompt provision of a mechanical ventilator in the event of ventilatory failure is one aspect of the inhalation therapist's contribution to coordinated patient care.

former appellations "tank jockeys" and "oxygen orderlies" are virtually forgotten, and the inhalation therapist—member of a profession that continues to develop—has emerged as a trusted member of the health care team. (See Fig. 13.)

SCOPE OF PROFESSIONAL SERVICES

The functions of the contemporary inhalation therapist may be better understood by considering the services that inhalation therapy is able to offer to the members of one hypothetical family, the Hendersons.

Jimmy Henderson, a premature newborn infant at Children's Hospital, required prolonged and intensive services of the Inhalation Therapy Department. The drama began in the delivery room where the obstetrician resuscitated Jimmy by using a mask and collapsible oxygen bag, similar in design to those used by inhalation therapists when they regularly participate as members of the hospital's resuscitation team. Jimmy continued to exhibit labored and irregular breathing even after he was placed in an incubator, an apparatus permitting control of the temperature, humidity, and oxygen concentration of an infant's environment.

The inhalation therapist repeatedly obtained and analyzed samples of the infant's blood for oxygen and carbon dioxide partial pressures and noted that the level of carbon dioxide in Jimmy's blood was increasing. The attending physician then ordered that the infant be connected by means of a small nasal mask to a ventilator, a mechanical device that provides a variety of breathing patterns to the patient, thereby ensuring more efficient and less tiring ventilation. The Inhalation Therapy Department worked closely with nursing and medical personnel in observing Jimmy's progress and manipulating the ventilator as required. After six days the ventilator was no longer necessary, and the remainder of Jimmy's hospital stay was uneventful.

Deborah, the Hendersons' younger child, was born three years ago. Delivery was normal, but shortly after birth, she exhibited a slight degree of distressed breathing. At the obstetrician's order she was placed in an incubator. The inhalation therapist, in cooperation with the attending nurses, adjusted the unit's controls to provide the slight increase in oxygen that had been prescribed. By means of an oxygen analyzer, a member of the Inhalation Therapy Department checked and recorded the oxygen level initially once each half hour and then once every four hours thereafter throughout the two days that Deborah spent in the incubator.

The use of the manual resuscitation device, the mechanical ventilator, and the blood gas analyzer all have parallels in the techniques that inhalation therapists use to assist adult patients. Doug Henderson, Jimmy and Deborah's father, recently underwent surgery for removal of a lung tumor. His physician, aware that many patients of this type suffer postoperative respiratory complications, contacted the Inhalation Therapy Department at Community General Hospital. He requested that, in cooperation with the Physical Therapy Department, Mr. Henderson be given preoperative instructions about proper coughing techniques and possible intermittent mechanical ventilation. After his surgery Mr. Henderson developed an elevated temperature, and a chest film taken by the radiologic technologist showed atelectasis, or airlessness, of certain lung areas. Mr. Henderson's physician, judging that the intermittent positive pressure breathing device might cause the affected lung portions to reexpand, ordered it administered in conjunction with mucus-liquefying agents on an hourly basis by the inhalation therapist. Although no dramatic claims were made for the treatment, it is possible that the resources of the Inhalation Therapy Department and the skill of its staff contributed to the improvement in Mr. Henderson's condition and to decreasing the length of his hospital stay.

The profession's growing involvement in the general community was used to good effect by Frank Henderson, Doug Henderson's father. The area chapter of the American Association for Inhalation Therapy had arranged and staffed a community pulmonary screening program in cooperation with the local respiratory disease association and the chest physicians' society. Doug Henderson encouraged his father to go because the senior Mr. Henderson had complained for some time of being short of breath, and he had a cough that he had come to accept as normal—perhaps as the result of a lifetime of smoking. The inhalation therapist working in the program calculated the readings of Frank Henderson's ability to breath efficiently, as recorded on a device called a spirometer. When the doctor in charge interpreted these records he found indications that Mr. Henderson might be suffering from an obstructive lung disorder. Mr. Henderson was referred to Community General Hospital's outpatient respiratory service. Here the inhalation therapist, working with other health team members, used sophisticated laboratory procedures to carefully assess Mr. Henderson's condition. The inhalation therapist then instructed him in the use of inhaled aerosolized medications, appropriate personal care, and exercises intended to enhance his physical condition. Frank Henderson's lungs will never regain the efficiency they possessed prior to the shortsighted satisfaction of those early cigarettes, but, partly because of the expertise of the inhalation therapist, he now leads a more pleasant life than he had known for many years.

The foregoing family vignette illustrates more than a dozen aspects of the routine activities of inhalation therapists working in an up-to-the-minute respiratory service.

PROFESSIONAL LEVELS AND EDUCATION

Inhalation therapy requires different types of personnel with varying levels of training and preparation. Inhalation therapy assistants or aides receive on-the-job training at hospitals that are able to support effective programs of in-service education. Inexperienced personnel are hired as trainees, and learn to perform the duties of inhalation therapy assistants or aides. During their training they are also paid employees. Many people presently active in the field began in just this way, although in recent years other avenues have opened for those interested in professional advancement. Inhalation therapy technicians are usually personnel who have completed an educational program designed to prepare them to apply for certification by the AAIT prior to their employment.

Inhalation therapists must successfully complete a more rigorous course of study. Although there are several routes for those who want to become registered inhalation therapists, the most common approach is through the AMA-approved course of study. This curriculum, in addition to or concurrent with at least two years of college, requires no less than 1,800 clock hours of study, two thirds of which are devoted to aspects of clinical practice under supervision. The remaining course work covers basic sciences and technical theory and their application to various medical specialties. For example, a student may study the principles of fluid mechanics in a physics course, examine their application in the interface between a human lung system and a mechanical ventilator, and further observe and practice clinical application in work with pulmonary medical and surgical patients.

The prospective student may select one of approximately eighty schools whose programs have received AMA approval. Other schools are presently involved in the accrediting process. Recently the field has become even more open-ended with the establishment of some programs at the baccalaureate level. These not only offer a broad technical and science foundation but also prepare interested students for careers in teaching, research, or administration in related fields and provide the groundwork for graduate study in these areas. Requirements for admission vary among schools, but the community college affiliated programs in particular offer extremely reasonable entrance requirements in line with their open-door admissions policies. Students are more readily accepted into a program if they have a good science background as well as a high school diploma.

EMPLOYMENT OPPORTUNITIES

At the present time, graduates in inhalation therapy are most likely to locate (after a one-year period of professional employment that separates their actual graduation from the time when they take the National Registration Examination) in a general or pediatric hospital facility, where they work in either the inhalation therapy department, a pulmonary laboratory setting, or both. Increasingly, however, well-qualified therapists are preparing themselves to enter the ranks of technical educators. The range of vocational opportunities for persons technically competent in matters of respiratory dysfunction is certainly still growing.

Although salaries do vary from region to region, in accordance with the size of the employing facility and because of rapid professional growth, the newly graduated inhalation therapist may reasonably expect to begin employment at a salary comparable to, or in excess of, that of a graduate nurse. The registered inhalation therapist may initially receive from $8,000 to $10,000 annually.

SUMMARY

This has been a brief look at an allied medical profession so young and malleable that a change in the name of the national association is even now being considered. The growth of the profession has been so swift that standards for educational programs are being reviewed for a second time, despite the fact that they were initiated only eight years ago. Even as problems of human interaction with the respirable environment continue to mount, this new breed of technician is developing to meet the challenge.

BIBLIOGRAPHY

Collins, V. J.: Inhalation therapy education and programs, J.A.M.A. **207:**329, 1969.

Egan, D. F.: Inhalation therapy department: staffing and services, Hospitals **42:**40, 1968.

Egan, D. F.: Fundamentals of inhalation therapy, ed. 1, St. Louis, 1969, The C. V. Mosby Co.

Eisenberg, L.: History of inhalation therapy equipment, Int. Anesth. Clin. 4:549, 1966.

Gingrich, G. D.: Inhalation therapy service, Hosp. Manage. 107:36, 55, 1969.

Inhalation Therapy, published monthly by the American Association for Inhalation Therapy.

Miller, W. F.: Respiratory therapy: what does it offer? Anesth. Analg. 47:599, 1968.

Petty, T. L., and Nett, L. M.: For those who live and breathe with emphysema and chronic bronchitis, Springfield, Ill., 1967, Charles C Thomas, Publisher.

PROFESSIONAL ORGANIZATIONS WHERE FURTHER INFORMATION CAN BE OBTAINED:

American Association for Inhalation Therapy
3554 Ninth Street
Riverside, California 92501

American Registry of Inhalation Therapists, Inc.
c/o University of Rochester
School of Medicine
Rochester, New York 14620

Chapter 12

MEDICAL RECORD ADMINISTRATION

Daniel J. Pae

Hospital record keeping is an important facet of effective health care. Medical record administration is an exciting and relatively new field (forty years old) that is becoming increasingly important in the age of technology and computerized data storage.

MEDICAL RECORDS

A medical record is a permanent history of a patient's illness or injury. Its purpose is to assist in his treatment as well as to compile in an orderly, complete, and accurate document all pertinent information of medical, scientific, and legal importance. Medical records contain the observations and findings noted by physicians in written communications and reports as well as data compiled by all involved hospital departments. In addition to the patient's medical history, each record contains diagnostic information, reports on his progress toward recovery and rehabilitation while he is in the hospital, x-ray films and laboratory reports, prescribed medication and diets, cardiogram tracings, pathology reports, and other essential medical information. Medical records are kept by hospitals, clinics, nursing homes, and medical research centers.

Computers are playing an ever-growing role in the field of medicine. Many physicians are using computers as an aid in diagnosis. Cardiograms can now be read and blood samples can be analyzed almost instantly by the computer. Hospitals have been using computers for many years to compile medical record statistics. Much valuable medical record information is currently stored in computers, and the medical record administrator must understand how computerization assists in patient care by providing medical record information at a moment's notice.

NEED FOR MEDICAL RECORDS

The work of the medical record administrator is of vital importance to many people. A medical record is often essential to the accurate diagnosis and rapid treatment of a patient's illness. It

Fig. 14. Medical records keep the physician informed concerning the care being provided by other members of the health care team.

serves as an immediate source of information to physicians as well as to all other health professionals involved in the patient's care and treatment. (See Fig. 14.) Medical records, made available to the doctor at a moment's notice, keep him informed concerning the care being provided by others and give him necessary information if the patient should be readmitted. The following case study illustrates the importance of having such information immediately available.

> Mrs. W. came to the hospital emergency room at 11:35 P.M. complaining of severe abdominal pain. Since she had been a patient at the hospital during the previous week, the emergency room physician called the Medical Record Department to request her medical record. The appropriate medical record number was obtained from the computerized master file and within one minute Mrs. W.'s previous medical record was on the way to the emergency room, where it was carefully reviewed. The medical record described the surgery that had been performed on Mrs. W. and listed the medications she was receiving. This information facilitated the diagnosis and treatment of Mrs. W.'s acute problem. Possibly it might even have helped to save her life.

Public health officials use medical records to determine community health conditions and disease trends. The prevention and control of epidemics often depend upon the availability of complete, up-to-date medical information. In addition, many important medical discoveries have resulted from a careful study of medical records, for they provide the medical researcher with a starting point for the development of new methods for the prevention, diagnosis, and treatment of disease, as shown in the following case study.

> The Department of Surgery at a large city hospital conducted a retrospective review of all cases of acute pancreatitis ever treated there. The Medical Record Department reviewed its disease index, obtained the medical record numbers of all of these cases, and retrieved the records from the stacks. Almost 1,500 medical records were reviewed in this intensive study, and valuable information was compiled on alternate methods of treatment of acute pancreatitis.

Medical records are frequently used in verifying insurance claims and in authenticating legal documents, as shown in this next case study.

> Mrs. M. was admitted to the hospital as a result of an automobile accident in which she suffered facial lacerations and a severely injured back. After plastic surgery on her face and treatment of her back injury that included surgery, physical therapy, and a brace, she was discharged from the hospital. Later Mrs. M.'s accident claim came up in court. The hospital received a *subpoena duces tecum* for her medical record, requiring that it be brought before the court. The medical record administrator took the witness stand and testified that this was indeed Mrs. M.'s medical record, that it had been in the continuous custody of the hospital, and that it had not been altered or tampered with. Because the information contained in Mrs. M.'s medical record substantiated her claims, she received compensation for the injuries she had received in the accident.

Hospital administrators also depend on information in these carefully compiled records to help establish or correct hospital policies and plan accurately for the future.

ROLE OF THE MEDICAL RECORD ADMINISTRATOR

The medical record administrator is responsible for organizing and supervising the medical record department so that it will function smoothly and efficiently in all of the following areas:

1. *Gathering and organizing information on each patient.* This information must be obtained from each member of the professional staff. The medical record administrator must plan effective medical record systems and design effective forms upon which to record pertinent information.
2. *Maintaining an information-retrieval system.* It is essential that medical records be made available with economy of time and effort. In many hospitals, computer systems are now being used for this aspect of medical record administration.
3. *Releasing information to authorized persons.* If a patient needs emergency treatment, his previous medical records must be available to his physician at a minute's notice. Health officials, insurance companies, and law courts often depend upon medical records for accurate, up-to-date information.
4. *Analyzing information for future use.* Thousands of statistics pour into the medical record department every day. These are compiled and made available to doctors, hospital administrators, public health officials, and health planning personnel.

HOW TO BECOME A MEDICAL RECORD ADMINISTRATOR

Men and women who want to become professional registered record librarians must successfully complete a program in medical record administration at a school approved by the AMA. There are presently two types of approved programs: (1) a college or university undergraduate program leading to a baccalaureate degree with a major in medical record administration or (2) a postgraduate program (available to those who have already earned a baccalaureate degree) that requires twelve months of study to earn a certificate in medical record administration. A graduate of either approved program is required to pass the national registration examination of the American Medical Record Association (AMRA) in order to become a registered record librarian (R.R.L.).

COURSES REQUIRED FOR MEDICAL RECORD ADMINISTRATION

In addition to meeting basic education requirements in the liberal arts, medical record administration students take courses in anatomy and physiology, medical terminology, medical record science, statistics, medical law, administration, and computer science. The curricula may vary slightly from school to school.

JOB OPPORTUNITIES

The demand for competent medical record administrators far exceeds the supply, and as a result, not all accredited hospitals and clinics have these trained professionals. Because of the increasing number of hospitals, clinics, and nursing homes and the growing volume and complexity of hospital records, there appears to be no end to the shortage of medical record administrators during the 1970s. Salaries are commensurate with those paid to other health professionals with comparable training, although salaries are largely dependent upon the size and location of the hospital, medical center, or government agency. Many organizations that employ medical record administrators also offer generous employee benefits.

PROFESSIONAL STATUS

Registered record librarians are entitled to professional status. They may serve as department heads with the same status as directors of other departments such as nursing, dietetics, or physical therapy. They are often required to attend staff meetings where medical records may be used to help establish hospital policies.

PERSONAL QUALIFICATIONS

Students considering careers in medical record administration should have a natural aptitude for precision work and for detail. They must be responsible, discreet, and tactful, using poise and patience to deal with busy, hard-pressed physicians as well as worried patients and their families. Medical record administrators, like physicians, must at all times be bound by the necessity for accuracy and confidentiality. In addition, they must be able to master technical and medical terminology.

SUPPORTIVE PERSONNEL

The medical record administrator is assisted by medical record technicians, who are responsible for analyzing medical records, working with file clerks, compiling information for statistics, and preparing reports for the medical record administrator. There are two ways to become an accredited medical record technician (A.R.T.). Many junior colleges offer associate degree programs that qualify applicants for the national accreditation examination. The

AMRA also offers a correspondence course that qualifies students for the same examination. These accredited medical record technicians are valuable assistants to the medical record administrator.

SUMMARY

The medical record administrator might be termed the scorekeeper of the medical team. There is a never-ending need for medical records not only in patient care but also in community health. Medical record data are received from a variety of health professionals. It is the responsibility of medical record administrators to organize a system of record keeping, design forms to contain the desired information, and maintain an efficient filing and retrieval system. They analyze and evaluate records, compile health statistics, and work with many groups and committees concerned with health care. A career as a medical record administrator offers these advantages:

1. The opportunity to provide skilled service to the public as well as to other health professionals
2. Membership in a young and rapidly expanding profession that offers status and prestige to qualified members
3. Financial security based on good salary levels supplemented by employee benefits
4. The challenge of being part of the endless drama of hospital life

BIBLIOGRAPHY

Horizons unlimited, ed. 8, Chicago, 1970, American Medical Association, p. 106.
Medical Record News, published bi-monthly by the American Medical Record Association.

PROFESSIONAL ORGANIZATION WHERE FURTHER INFORMATION CAN BE OBTAINED:

American Medical Record Association
875 North Michigan Avenue
Suite 1850 John Hancock Center
Chicago, Illinois 60611

Chapter 13

MEDICAL TECHNOLOGY

Marjorie L. Brunner

Medical technology is one of the newest and fastest growing professions associated with modern advances in medical science. Medical technologists work in clinical pathology laboratories performing the scientific tests that track down the cause and cure of disease. Some diseases, diabetes and leukemia for example, can be positively identified by laboratory methods alone. The presence of other suspected diseases can be confirmed by laboratory examination.

Medical technologists are prepared to function not only as laboratory workers but also as supervisors, instructors, and researchers. They are educated and technically trained to perform the various chemical, microscopic, bacteriologic, and other medical laboratory procedures used in the diagnosis, study, and treatment of disease. Medical technologists work under the supervision of a pathologist, a physician who specializes in laboratory medicine.

HOW DID MEDICAL TECHNOLOGY DEVELOP?

In the early days of clinical laboratory science, pathologists, who were just beginning to receive recognition as necessary and important medical specialists in their own right, performed their own laboratory tests. As the field of laboratory medicine developed and broadened, pathologists found it necessary to train assistants to help perform the simpler tests. The profession of medical technology thus came into being in the early part of this century.

In those years, high school graduates interested in medical technology commonly became apprentices in medical laboratories. Then a few commercial schools were established, but the training they offered was often inadequate, and their fees were usually exorbitant. Realizing that laboratory medicine was developing rapidly and that standards had to be established for the training of laboratory assistants, the American Society of Clinical Pathologists (ASCP) established the Board of Registry of Medical Technologists in 1928 and elected six pathologists to serve on the Board. The Registry administers the national certification examination to prospective medical technologists after they complete all educational requirements. The first certificates were issued in 1930.

The American Society of Medical Technologists (ASMT) was organized in 1933. Membership was restricted to medical technologists certified by the Board of Registry. The present ASMT membership totals approximately 16,500.

Today the Board of Registry of Medical Technologists consists of six members of ASCP and five members of ASMT. By gradually elevating educational standards and improving the quality of technical training, both the Board of Registry and ASMT have done much to raise the status of medical laboratory workers to a professional level.

WHERE DO MEDICAL TECHNOLOGISTS WORK? WHAT ARE THEIR CONTRIBUTIONS TO HEALTH CARE?

Clinical pathology laboratories, where most medical technologists are employed, include a variety of specialized areas. In the blood bank the medical technologist's knowledge and skill in matching blood samples are crucial. In addition to the familiar testing for blood groups and Rh factors, verifying that the patient's blood sample is compatible with the donor's blood can require from six to twenty highly sensitive and specific determinations.

In microbiology the greatest amount of work involves bacteria. The technologists grow and identify bacteria present in biological specimens obtained from patients and do tests to help determine which antibiotics will be most effective in subduing the organism causing the infection. (See Fig. 15.)

Problems in parasitology center on the search for and identification of parasites—the small animals living inside the body. These may be tapeworms or pinworms, or they may be tiny one-celled animals such as the parasite that causes malaria.

A knowledge of chemistry is used in many ways in medical laboratories. Technologists determine the presence and quantity of chemical substances in blood and other body fluids obtained from patients. Comparisons of the chemical constituents of patient specimens with normal values established in specimens from healthy individuals provide useful guides for the physician in his diagnosis and control of disease.

In serology the medical technologist uses standardized techniques to demonstrate the presence and amount of antibodies or

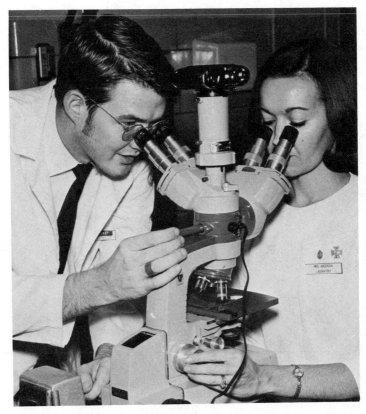

Fig. 15. Technologists in a microbiology laboratory examine a patient's specimen for the presence of bacteria.

antibody-like substances in body fluids such as serum, plasma, spinal fluid, and urine. In many instances the production of these substances by the body has been stimulated by an infection or by immunization. The Widal test, for example, demonstrates the presence of serum antibodies to *Salmonella typhosa,* which is the causative agent of typhoid fever.

Analyses of urine samples are beneficial in diagnosing or controlling illnesses caused by malfunction of the kidneys. Examination of urine specimens gives clues to such diseases as nephritis and diabetes. A potential new application for these tests is emerging through research into the biochemical conditions that are related to mental disorders.

In hematology, tests are conducted to detect conditions that

111

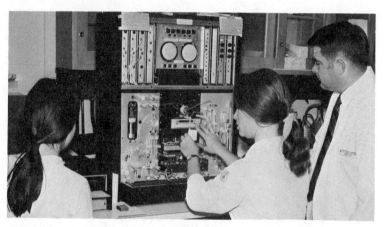

Fig. 16. Precision instruments are used to increase the accuracy and speed of blood counts performed in the hematology laboratory.

primarily affect the blood, such as anemia (a deficiency of red blood cells commonly known as tired blood), hemophilia (a disease in which the blood clotting mechanism is defective), and leukemia (a type of cancer involving an abnormal increase in the number of white blood cells). (See Fig. 16.)

Work in a medical laboratory requires the use of a wide array of intricate precision equipment—microscopes, automatic analyzers that permit an increased number of patient fluid samples to be chemically analyzed with greater speed and accuracy, and electronic counters used for the enumeration of red and white blood cells. Specialized procedures such as electrophoresis and gas chromatography are used to isolate compounds present in body fluids so they may be identified and quantitated. New instruments and methods of analysis are constantly being developed, so that medical technologists are involved in an atmosphere of continuous learning, evaluation, and progress.

The types of positions available to the medical technologist are as varied as the many tests they perform. Laboratory work is being done in hospitals, clinics, doctors' offices, public health departments, and private research institutes as well as in industry. Those who prefer to watch the results of their work as it affects the health of specific individuals would probably prefer a position in a small hospital, clinic, or doctor's office, where they have an opportunity to get acquainted with the people they help. Other technologists may choose to work in research or industry, where their contributions may one day have a far-reaching effect on the health of many people.

Research positions that involve primarily routine laboratory techniques are often filled by supporting laboratory personnel such as certified laboratory assistants. However, research positions involving the development of new laboratory methods, the adaptation of existing methods to new equipment, and the evaluation of technical problems are available to experienced technologists in many clinical laboratories. Occasionally, experienced technologists or those with advanced education work in basic research, an area that requires a good deal of initiative and independent thinking. They work closely with consultant pathologists or specialists in a related scientific field.

The following case study illustrates the contribution a medical technologist might make to the study, diagnosis, and treatment of a patient.

A 30-year-old expectant mother was seen by an obstetrician for prenatal care. Her medical history revealed that this was her fourth pregnancy. Her blood type was recorded as A, Rh negative, and her husband's blood type was O, Rh positive. Her first pregnancy had occurred when she was 23 years of age, and her baby was delivered after a full term of 40 weeks' gestation. The baby's blood type was O, Rh positive, and he was unaffected by the incompatibility of his parents' Rh factors. During the patient's second pregnancy, when she was 25 years of age, Rh antibodies present in her blood passed through the placenta into the baby's circulatory system, where they reacted with and destroyed some of the baby's red blood cells. The infant was delivered after 40 week's gestation and was given a blood transfusion to replenish his red blood cells. He responded well to this treatment. The patient's third pregnancy occurred at the age of 26 years. An Rh incompatibility was again apparent. The baby was given a blood transfusion after delivery at 40 weeks' gestation, but he failed to respond to this treatment and died soon after birth.

With this background information the obstetrician began to study his patient's condition. He requested that a medical technologist obtain blood samples from the patient and her husband to confirm their blood types. The medical technologist in the blood bank determined the patient's type as A, Rh negative, and the husband's type as O, Rh positive. The technologist also detected the presence of antibodies against the Rh factor in the patient's blood and determined further that the antibody level was significant.

At 24 weeks' gestation the obstetrician collected a specimen of the amniotic fluid in which the baby was floating. This specimen was sent to the clinical laboratory, where another medical technologist performed a test that indicated the amount of red blood cell destruction present in the baby. This test was repeated at 26 weeks of gestation and again at 27 weeks because it seemed that the baby's condition was deteriorating. During the twenty-eighth week of gestation the obstetrician and pathologist decided that laboratory results of the amniotic fluid tests indicated the need for an intrauterine transfusion. Compatible blood was found and cross-matched by the medical technologist. The baby received a total of three transfusions in utero at 28, 30, and 32 weeks' gestation. Amniotic fluid was collected just prior to each transfusion. Part of this fluid was sent to the clinical bacteriology laboratory, where the medical technologist inoculated it onto media that would enhance the growth of any microorganisms present. Fortunately there were no indications of intrauterine infection.

At 36 weeks' gestation, labor was induced, and when the baby was delivered, blood samples were immediately collected from his umbilical cord and sent to the clinical laboratory. The medical technologist in the hematology laboratory performed blood cell counts and hemoglobin measurements to determine the degree of anemia present, and the medical technologist in the clinical chemistry laboratory made repeated measurements of the amount of bilirubin present in the blood. This is a compound produced by red blood cell destruction, and it can cause brain damage in the newborn infant if it is present in the blood in large quantities. Fortunately the level of bilirubin in this child's blood was only moderately elevated, and further blood transfusions were not necessary due to the protection the child had received through the intrauterine transfusions.

WHAT ARE THE EDUCATIONAL REQUIREMENTS?

Educational requirements for medical technology include a minimum of three years of college plus twelve months of clinical training in one of the 773 hospital laboratory schools of medical technology accredited by the Council on Medical Education of the AMA. Since January 1, 1962, the pretechnical educational requirements for admission to an approved school of medical technology have been three years (90 semester hours or 135 quarter hours) of course work in any accredited college or university. The student's program must include the following credits:

1. A minimum of sixteen semester hours (twenty-four quarter hours) of chemistry

2. A minimum of sixteen semester hours (twenty-four quarter hours) of biological science
3. A minimum of one semester or quarter of college-level mathematics

The college or university should accept this course work as the first three years of a baccalaureate program in medical technology. Some of the approved schools of medical technology have their own specific course requirements in addition to those mentioned.

After earning the necessary college credits, students must satisfactorily complete a course of instruction in all phases of medical technology at an approved school. Major topics of instruction include hematology, urinalysis, clinical microbiology, serology, blood banking, and clinical chemistry. After completing these professional education requirements, students are eligible for the baccalaureate degree. In order to become registered medical technologists—M.T.(ASCP)—students must pass the examination administered by the Board of Registry of Medical Technologists.

There are also advanced educational programs for medical technologists who wish to specialize in one particular field. For example, the certification program of the American Association of Blood Banks is designed to train specialists in blood banking. This program is offered only by institutions that have been approved by the Association and consists of one year of training. This program includes both didactic study and practical experience and is designed to provide a comprehensive education in all aspects of the modern-day blood bank. After completing the course, all candidates for certification must take the examination that is given once each year by the Board of Registry of Medical Technologists (ASCP) in cooperation with the Committee on Education of the American Association of Blood Banks. The examination consists of written and practical portions, and both must be passed in the same year. The technologist then becomes a certified blood bank specialist— M.T.(ASCP)B.B. There are also certification programs in bacteriology and clinical chemistry. Since these specialists are expected to have a wide range of competence and a thorough understanding of their particular fields, they often become supervisors, work on advanced research projects, or in special reference laboratories.

Students planning a career in medical technology should consider the possibility of pursuing a graduate degree. Graduate education is assuming increasing importance as necessary preparation for the more interesting job opportunities. It is also becoming more feasible for the average student because of the increased availability of financial aid. Information concerning graduate programs in medical technology is available through the Board of Schools of Medical Technology (ASCP).

WHAT PARTICULAR QUALITIES ARE NEEDED?

A list of qualifications for a career in medical technology might include an interest in science, an active curiosity, a bent for accuracy, and a general desire to help mankind. Self-discipline, a spirit of cooperation, and thorough moral and intellectual integrity are essential in the practice of this profession. The laboratory findings obtained by medical technologists are used in making vital decisions concerning human lives. Therefore procedures must be performed with accuracy and the result evaluated with the utmost integrity.

WHO ARE THE SUPPORTING PROFESSIONALS IN MEDICAL LABORATORIES?

There are many workers in medical laboratories whose educational backgrounds are more limited than those of medical technologists. Nonetheless, they are trained to perform necessary and valuable services in the laboratory. Certified laboratory assistants are capable of handling a variety of procedures under the supervision of a medical technologist. Their tasks may range from collecting blood specimens to operating modern and complex equipment. Educational requirements for certified laboratory assistants include a diploma from an accredited high school plus twelve months of training in an AMA-approved hospital school for certified laboratory assistants. Training includes lectures and applied laboratory training, and students who complete the program are eligible to take the national examination given by the Board of Certified Laboratory Assistants (ASCP). Those who pass the examination become certified laboratory assistants—C.L.A.(ASCP).

A second supporting professional in a medical laboratory is the cytotechnologist. Cytotechnologists are concerned with cytology, the science of cells, and are trained to recognize those minute abnormalities in the size, shape, and color of cell substances that may signal the presence of cancer. Their main tool is the microscope, and a variety of special stains are used to accentuate cell patterns. Cytotechnologists must complete two years of college, including twelve semester hours in biology, plus twelve months of training at one of nearly 100 schools of cytotechnology approved by the AMA. After candidates pass the examination given by the

Board of Registry of Medical Technologists, they become cyto-technologists—C.T.(ASCP).

Histologic technicians are also members of the medical labora-tory team. They prepare portions of selected body tissues for microscopic examination. Tissue preparation involves freezing and cutting tissue samples into ultrathin slices, mounting them on slides, and staining them with special dyes to make cell details more clearly visible under the microscope. Histologic technicians must have a high school diploma plus one year of supervised training in a qualified pathology laboratory. After certification through exami-nation by the Board of Registry of Medical Technologists, histologic technicians are given the designation H.T.(ASCP).

Medical laboratory technicians are the most recently estab-lished category of supporting professionals in a medical laboratory. The level of responsibility that can be assumed by the medical laboratory technician lies between that of the certified laboratory assistant and the medical technologist. Two-year programs leading to an associate degree for medical laboratory technicians are pres-ently being established. Certification as medical laboratory tech-nicians—M.L.T.(ASCP)—is available to those who successfully complete the certification examination given by the Board of Reg-istry (ASCP).

WHAT CAN LABORATORY PERSONNEL EXPECT TO EARN?

Starting salaries earned by laboratory personnel vary accord-ing to the level of their training and performance and are also determined in part by the size of the employing facility and its geographical location. Beginning medical technologists earn from $6,500 to $8,500 annually. Cytotechnologists without bachelor of science degrees may expect to earn from $4,750 to $6,250 a year; these same personnel with a degree will start at annual salaries ranging from $6,500 to $8,500. Medical laboratory technologists and histologic technicians earn annual starting salaries of $4,750 to $6,250, and beginning certified laboratory assistants are paid from $4,400 to $5,800 a year.

WHAT IS THE DEMAND FOR MEDICAL TECHNOLOGISTS?

A career in medical technology is both stimulating and reward-ing. Although a majority of the 70,500 ASCP-registered medical technologists are women, the number of men entering the profes-sion is increasing rapidly. The growing dependence on laboratory tests in the diagnosis and treatment of disease as well as the construction of more hospital and medical facilities have increased the demand for medical technologists. It is estimated that 90,000 professional medical technologists will be needed by 1978. Registered medical technologists will find excellent opportunities for employment in every part of the country.

BIBLIOGRAPHY

The Registry of Medical Technologists of the American Society of Clinical Pathologists, Chicago, 1969, Board of Registry of Medical Technologists, American Society of Clinical Pathologists.

What kind of a career could I have in a medical laboratory? Chicago, no date, Board of Registry of Medical Technologists, American Society of Clinical Pathologists.

PROFESSIONAL ORGANIZATIONS WHERE FURTHER INFORMATION CAN BE OBTAINED:

American Society of Clinical Pathologists
710 South Wolcott Avenue
Chicago, Illinois 60612

American Society of Medical Technologists
Suite 1600, Hermann Professional Building
Houston, Texas 77025

Chapter 14

OCCUPATIONAL THERAPY

Scott Worley and C. Kay Buckey

HISTORY OF OCCUPATIONAL THERAPY

The beneficial effects of physical and mental activity (occupation) have long been recognized. It was not until this century, however, that selected activities were used to reduce the effects of illness by meeting the specific needs of an individual patient. During World War I, occupational therapists trained in the United States were sent to assist soldiers who had been wounded and were convalescing in Europe. This was the beginning of occupational therapy as it is known today. These early training programs were established in conjunction with hospitals. The many soldiers wounded or otherwise disabled as a result of World War II required skilled assistance, and this demand provided additional stimulus for the growth of occupational therapy. Educational programs became university or college affiliated, and graduate programs were developed to meet the increasing need for more highly skilled therapists.

PROFESSIONAL FUNCTIONS

Occupational therapy is a profession concerned with helping the patient to achieve optimal development of his physical and emotional abilities. In their work, occupational therapists evaluate each patient's particular physical and psychological needs and then develop and prescribe a treatment program designed to meet them. They then determine the appropriate attitudes and techniques necessary for effective treatment. (See Fig. 17.) An understanding of medical information and human behavior, keen and perceptive observation, and recognition of individual needs make it possible for an occupational therapist to build a cooperative relationship in which both therapist and patient strive to attain the patient's highest level of performance. Therapists must discover which of the patient's specific physical and emotional needs are amenable to treatment through his activity, and they must understand the mean-

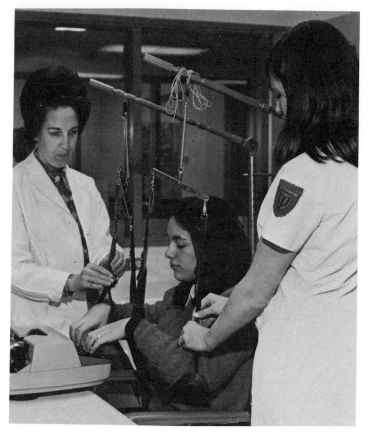

Fig. 17. A patient with partial paralysis of the arms is evaluated to determine if slings or other supports will allow her to type.

ing and dynamics of specific tasks from the cultural standpoint as well as from the perspective of the individual patient. These tasks are frequently indistinguishable from activities of the patient's normal daily life.

The occupational therapist works with patients individually and in groups, using a variety of creative, educational, industrial, manual, musical, prevocational, and recreational activities to enhance motor function and promote psychological, social, and economic adjustment. Teaching patients to regain daily living skills through the use of artificial limbs, assistive devices, or special equipment is an additional responsibility of the therapist. (See Fig. 18.)

Fig. 18. Occupational therapist guides hyperkinetic child in assembling a toy manikin to aid in developing eye-hand coordination and perceptual skills.

As a member of the rehabilitation team, the occupational therapist plans and works cooperatively with nurses, physical therapists, and vocational counselors to help patients achieve their highest potential. The patients may be of any age and may suffer from cardiac or neurological impairment, arthritis, physical injury, mental retardation, emotional disturbance or virtually any disability. Occupational therapists work in a variety of settings, including children's hospitals, general hospitals, rehabilitation centers, psychiatric clinics, special schools, sheltered workshops, services for the homebound, and other community agencies. Some therapists, working in conjunction with qualified referring physicians, establish their own practices. The following case study illustrates some of the contributions an occupational therapist can make to patient care.

Janet, who is 5 years of age, participates very normally now in her kindergarten class, using her prosthetic right arm nearly as efficiently as she would have used her own hand. At the age of $2^1/_2$ years, Janet was involved in an automobile accident. Her injuries resulted in the amputation of her right arm. Because of head injuries, she was unconscious for nearly a week. Her mother, who had been driving when the accident occurred, also had a very difficult adjustment period afterward. Occupational therapy played an important role in both Janet's recovery and her mother's readjustment.

The occupational therapist who was providing an environmental stimulation program of many different tactile, auditory, and olfactory stimuli was the first to discover the child's returning consciousness and was able to enhance it through adjustment of the stimulation program. During the early stages of Janet's recovery the occupational therapist also carefully evaluated the nature of her play and used some specific tests to determine whether there were any problems of motor coordination or perception as a result of her injuries. Fortunately, no problems were noted, and consequently that portion of the occupational therapy program designed to encourage Janet's normal development with play and interaction with other children was not complicated.

Even before the little girl was first fitted with a prosthesis and brought to the Occupational Therapy Department for training in its use, her therapist had already made important contributions to the prosthetic and amputee evaluation team by providing vital information about Janet's level of development at play and in other activities. The therapist had also participated in deciding when the prosthesis should be provided and selecting the type of prosthesis to be used.

When she began to work with her occupational therapist, Janet quickly learned to use the device as a part of the daily play and self-care activities that the therapist had specifically designed for training purposes. She had no difficulty in learning to use subsequent prostheses that were prescribed as she grew. The occupational therapist checked out the mechanical and functional efficiency of each new prosthesis, and when Janet received the last one, she suggested an adjustment in the placement of a strap so Janet could put on the prosthesis more easily by herself. During this period the therapist was in close contact with Janet's family, suggesting toys and play activities that were appropriate for her level of interest as a growing, active child and that would also help her to develop more skill in using her prosthesis in self-care.

Janet's mother had not been physically injured in the accident, but because she had been driving the car, she was initially unable to adjust emotionally and held herself responsible for her daughter's injuries. She therefore received psychiatric help on an outpatient basis, and occupational therapy was part of her treatment. In that setting the occupational therapist's evaluation of how Janet's mother dealt with the tasks provided and with the other people in the treatment setting was used extensively in conjunction with specific evaluative procedures to guide further treatment. The ability of Janet's mother to function in her daily relationships was assessed on the basis of her response in these situations. The tasks and group situations in occupational therapy were carefully controlled and provided Janet's mother with an opportunity to handle her feelings of guilt, depression, and worthlessness. This treatment facilitated eventual discharge from the outpatient program.

Close communication was maintained between the two therapists working with Janet and her mother in order to prevent complications and facilitate the treatment of both mother and daughter.

Even though she is now doing well in kindergarten, Janet will probably be receiving occupational therapy in the future. Each time she needs a larger prosthesis, occupational therapy will make a contribution, and hopefully complications and adjustment problems will be minimal as she grows into adulthood.

LEVELS OF PERSONNEL

Registered occupational therapists (O.T.R.) are professionally qualified graduates of occupational therapy programs that are accredited by the AMA in collaboration with the American Occupational Therapy Association (AOTA). They have successfully completed the national registration examination and maintain registered membership in the AOTA. The therapist functions at a level that may involve supervision, administration, and consultation in addition to the evaluation, planning, and execution of treatment programs. The roles assumed by individual therapists depend upon their qualifications, areas of competence, and interests.

Educational requirements of approved occupational therapy curricula are geared to fulfilling the requirements for program accreditation. In addition to meeting certain specified minimum standards, each approved program must provide instruction in the behavioral and biological sciences, pathology (related to both emotional and physical problems), therapeutic techniques, and the theory of occupational therapy (related to psychiatry and physical dysfunction). These courses cover the physical and emotional needs of people of all ages. Currently the various accredited curricula include courses in the biological or physical sciences, or both and in English, psychology, and sociology.

Those interested in becoming registered occupational therapists may take one of three basic approaches. First, students may enroll at a college or university that offers an accredited occupational therapy program at the baccalaureate level. A second approach may be through occupational therapy curricula offering eighteen- to twenty-two-month programs for college graduates who have received baccalaureate degrees in related fields. There are a limited number of these programs, and they provide a certificate in occupational therapy, making those who complete the course eligible to take the national registration examination. These curricula should not be confused with the programs for certified occupational therapy assistants that are described later in this chapter. The third approach involves basic preparation in occupational therapy at the graduate level. The number of these programs is increasing, and they offer masters' degrees in occupational therapy for persons with undergraduate majors in biology, psychology, sociology, or other fields related to occupational therapy.

There are an increasing number of graduate programs designed to permit registered occupational therapists to do advanced work in preparation for specialized clinical practice or teaching in occupational therapy programs.

After they successfully complete an accredited occupational therapy curriculum and an approved program of clinical experience (varying from six months to one year in length) under the supervision of a practicing registered occupational therapist, graduates become eligible to take the registration examination of the AOTA. Successful completion of the examination admits them to the registry of occupational therapists and permits them to wear the insignia indicating registration.

Certified occupational therapy assistants (C.O.T.A.) function under the supervision of a registered occupational therapist in general activity, maintenance, and supportive programs of specific treatment. To become certified by the AOTA, it is necessary to complete an AOTA-approved training program and meet certification requirements.

These training programs include (1) studies of normal human structure, function, growth, and development; (2) studies of illness and injury and their effects on the patient; (3) experience with a variety of media used in occupational therapy; (4) principles and practice of occupational therapy; and (5) practical experience supervised by a registered occupational therapist.

Programs may vary in length from three months to two years, depending on the type of program and its location. Some two-year programs are offered by junior colleges. Graduates who meet the requirements may be employed as certified occupational therapy assistants, or they may receive some credit for transfer to a professional program at the baccalaureate level. Other programs are offered by vocational or technical schools, departments of adult education, or hospitals and other related agencies.

Programs may prepare the certified occupational therapy assistant to work with the mentally ill, geriatric patients, patients with chronic diseases, or in any of the major categories of patient care.

Some programs may restrict admission to people from a particular geographical area or have an employment requirement for admission. Therefore those who are interested in becoming certified occupational therapy assistants should check the requirements of specific programs.

Occupational therapy aides are trained on the job to meet the requirements and standards of the occupational therapy departments in which they work. They are directed or supervised by a registered therapist or certified occupational therapy assistant and may perform clerical, maintenance, or patient-related duties.

PROFESSIONAL ORGANIZATION

The American Occupational Therapy Association is the national organization of occupational therapists, and participation involves the professional, technical, and student levels of personnel within the profession. It is composed of local organizations (usually at the state level) that are affiliated with it and have representation in its policy-making body. The AOTA establishes standards within the profession and provides means of communication within the profession through newsletters and journals. The AOTA's goal is to foster educational and professional growth in the practice of occupational therapy.

PROFESSIONAL OPPORTUNITIES

There are not enough occupational therapists to fill all the positions available each year both in this country and abroad. In addition to direct contact with patients through treatment, therapists may be involved in research, teaching, consultation, and administration. The increasing national emphasis on health has opened many new frontiers of service, creating virtually limitless opportunities in this exciting and challenging profession.

Although salaries for occupational therapists vary according to geographical location, the beginning therapist might expect to earn a salary ranging from $7,500 to $8,500 annually. With experience and/or special training and education, therapists earn as much as $15,000 per year in settings that primarily provide treatment services. Those professionals who become educators, administrators, or consultants or who specialize in other areas may go beyond this range, depending on their education, experience, and competence.

BIBLIOGRAPHY

American Journal of Occupational Therapy, published monthly by the American Occupational Therapy Association.

Description of function in occupational therapy, New York, no date, American Occupational Therapy Association.

History of occupational therapy, Amer. J. Occup. Ther. 21 (5): entire issue, 1967.

Occupational therapy handbook, New York, 1969, American Occupational Therapy Association.

Reilly, M.: Occupational therapy can be one of the great ideas of 20th century medicine, Amer. J. Occup. Ther. 16:1, 1962.

Spackman, C. S.: A history of the practice of occupational therapy for the restoration of function for the physically disabled, Amer. J. Occup. Ther. 22:67, 1968.

The A-B-C's of occupational therapy, Greenfield, Mass., 1969, Channing L. Bete Co., Inc.

West, W.: Statement to the Committee on Health Manpower, Amer. J. Occup. Ther. 22:89, 1968.

Yerxa, E.: Authentic occupational therapy, Amer. J. Occup. Ther. 21:1, 1967.

PROFESSIONAL ORGANIZATION WHERE FURTHER INFORMATION CAN BE OBTAINED:

American Occupational Therapy Association
251 Park Avenue South
New York, New York 10010

Chapter 15

RADIOLOGIC TECHNOLOGY

Robert J. Bullock and Philip Ballinger

Almost every patient admitted to a hospital requires some type of an x-ray examination. This service may vary from a routine chest film to an elaborate study of one of the body systems that involves tremendously complicated and expensive equipment. Whether the examination is simple or complex, the final results will represent the combined efforts of the radiologist (a physician whose specialty is the use of x-rays and other radiation in diagnosis and treatment) and a radiologic technologist.

DEVELOPMENT OF THE PROFESSION

Few events have had as great an impact on the medical world as the discovery of x-rays in 1895. Physicians immediately realized the potential of this new energy that would allow them to see inside the patient. Therefore those with the necessary mechanical and technical abilities worked with physicists and other scientists, and within a year significant x-ray studies were being performed on patients.

The first radiographs (x-ray photographs) resulted from the combined efforts of physicians and physicists. At this stage the physicists operated crude x-ray generating equipment while the physician positioned the patient and evaluated the image on the finished glass plate. Soon x-ray equipment was being manufactured commercially, and more refined equipment became available.

As the practices of radiologists began to expand, they developed an increasing need for competent people who could take over much of the technical work involved in performing radiographic studies, allowing the radiologist to focus his efforts on the interpretation of films and other professional duties that must be performed by a physician.

Initially, office nurses served as radiologists' assistants, but as the science of radiology expanded, assistants needed more highly specialized skills. While physicians were developing the field of radiology as a medical specialty, x-ray technicians were being trained in the technical aspects of obtaining a radiograph. The introduction of radioactivity and the increased sophistication of therapeutic and diagnostic procedures required expanded educational programs. Through more demanding educational requirements and added responsibilities, these technical people were accumulating the knowledge and skills that distinguish today's radiologic technologists.

Since its inception the field of radiology has developed with remarkable rapidity. This progress has resulted from the development of new techniques by clinicians, mechanical and electronic contributions by the x-ray industry, and the continuing development and refinement of radiopaque contrast materials by the pharmaceutical industry.

The radiologist of the 1920s and 1930s studied images on a fluoroscopic screen—images so dim they could be seen only in a room that was totally dark. By the late 1950s, image intensifiers capable of increasing the brightness of the fluoroscopic image 6,000 times became available. This image intensifier now permits the use of television, motion picture cameras, and video tape to transmit or record studies of organs where motion is involved. This system can demonstrate the valves and blood vessels of the heart with great clarity, and it can also be used to great advantage for the more traditional studies of the gastrointestinal tract.

In certain respects the radiologic technologist is a representative of, as well as an assistant to, the radiologist. Radiologic examinations may be divided into two general categories: those performed by a radiologist because medical judgments are involved in the performance of the study and those in which the technologist produces radiographs that are later interpreted by a radiologist. In the latter case the patient will frequently be seen only by the technologist. This situation is particularly common in rural or small community hospitals where a radiologist may consult only on a part-time basis. Under these circumstances technologists must function with greater independence, judgment, and responsibility because they are often the only members of the health care team with any expertise in the field.

DIAGNOSTIC RADIOLOGY

When a patient is directed to the radiology department for a diagnostic examination, technologists prepare him by explaining

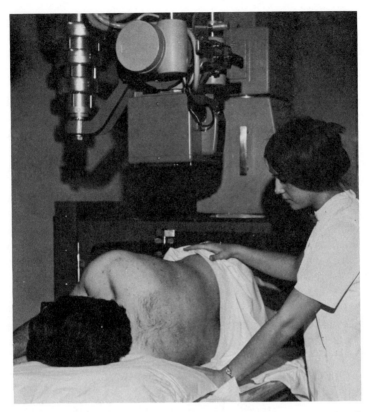

Fig. 19. Precise positioning of the patient is essential to produce a radiograph showing the detailed structure of the spine.

the procedures to be performed. They will then see that the patient is properly gowned and taken to the diagnostic room.

In order to obtain a radiograph, technologists must position the patient precisely to project the desired anatomical structures onto the film. To accomplish this they must relate external body landmarks to internal structures. (See Fig. 19.) The patient's weight, age, and physical condition must be evaluated in order that the proper x-ray exposure values can be selected. The film will then be exposed and sent to the darkroom to be processed by personnel under the technologist's supervision. Finished films are prepared for the radiologist's interpretation and are ultimately filed.

Radiologic technologists are responsible for patients during their stay in the radiology department, and some patients require considerable supportive care. In addition to working directly with patients, technologists must supervise the maintenance of equipment to assure dependable function, test new products, and maintain an appropriate stock of expendable supplies. In some institutions they may be called upon to develop new techniques to assist in research programs.

Radiologic technology can be thought of as an art, and in this respect it can be highly rewarding. A well-composed and properly exposed radiograph that clearly reveals the anatomy in question can appropriately be compared to an example of any of the graphic arts. In addition, technologists have the satisfaction of knowing that the information revealed will be essential to the patient's care and treatment. Personal satisfaction is also derived from performing difficult radiographic studies without causing additional discomfort to a patient who is already in pain. Radiographic examinations may range from relatively routine films to those urgently required in the emergency room or during surgery. In some cases, portable radiographic equipment is taken to the patient who cannot be moved to the radiology department.

The following case study illustrates the radiologic technologist's work in the emergency room, at the patient's bedside, in surgery, and in the radiology department—the main functions of the technologist in diagnostic radiology.

Mrs. H. fell down the front steps of her home and was taken to the hospital emergency room where she was examined by her physician. He detected a probable hip injury and directed a request for a hip study to the Radiology Department. Mrs. H. was taken to an x-ray room and carefully moved onto the radiographic table.

The technologist placed film in a tray under the radiographic table and moved the x-ray tube above the patient, centering it over her injured hip. The technologist was careful not to cause her further injury. After the initial exposure was made, the technologist moved the equipment so that a second projection could be made without moving the patient and risking additional pain and injury. Special devices were required to hold the second film at the patient's side, with the x-ray tube placed at right angles to the hip joint. Care was taken to move only the uninjured leg so that the injured area remained stationary. After the films were processed, the physician interpreted them and confirmed that Mrs. H.'s hip was fractured. Her physician informed her of the diagnosis; she was admitted to the orthopedic service and scheduled for surgery.

Immediately before the surgical repair of Mrs. H.'s hip was

begun, the radiologic technologist joined the other members of the surgical team in the operating room to take preliminary films. The exact position of the fractured hip was determined, the film was taken, and the surgeon used the radiograph as a point of reference in initiating surgery. He placed a guide wire into the fractured hip and the technologist took additional x-ray films. When the wire was satisfactorily located and did not require additional manipulation, the surgeon fixed the repair device to the fractured hip by sliding it over the guide wires. After the permanent pins or plates had been installed, the guide wire was removed and another series of radiographs were taken. Because the films showed satisfactory results, the surgeon was able to close the incision. Mrs. H. was kept under close observation during the days immediately following surgery and x-ray films were taken periodically to ensure that her hip had not moved. After her discharge from the hospital, Mrs. H. returned to the Radiology Department for additional "recheck" films. These radiographs told the surgeon how rapidly the hip was healing.

THERAPEUTIC RADIOLOGY

The therapeutic application of x-rays parallels the development of diagnostic radiology. The first therapeutic use of x-rays was reported in 1896. Since that time there has been a continuous development of higher energy generators and radioactive treatment sources with different and more effective modalities.

Technologists in radiotherapy work under the direction of a radiologist. They position the patient so that the radiation source and the area to be irradiated are in proper alignment. They regulate the controls of the radiation source to deliver the exact amount of radiation to be administered and observe the patient continually during the treatment period either through a television monitoring system or by directly viewing him through lead glass windows. Technologists also assist the physician in regular examinations of the patient to chart his progress. Assisting the radiologist in planning treatment programs is an interesting and challenging part of their activities. Many technologists prefer to work in therapeutic radiology because the longer association with a patient provides opportunities for technologists to see the results of their contributions to patient care.

NUCLEAR MEDICINE

Nuclear medicine, a product of the atomic age, is the third subspecialty of radiology. In this branch of medicine, radioactive isotopes are administered to the patient, whose body is then scanned with a device that detects radiation emitted from organs or areas where the isotope may have collected. The scanning device records the patterns of radioactivity on a film that the physician can use to diagnose tumors or other disease entities. In addition, tests of various biochemical and physiological functions are performed. Because the isotopes that are used are active for only a limited time, patients commonly experience no ill aftereffects.

Nuclear medicine technologists may prepare the selected isotope and administer it to a patient under the direction of a physician. They also operate the scanning device and produce the resultant scan film. People with a special interest in physics who enjoy precise laboratory work and complex instrumentation find this aspect of radiology especially attractive.

EDUCATIONAL PREPARATION

The American Association of Radiological Technicians, the first professional organization for allied health personnel in radiology, was founded in 1920. This organization, whose official title is now the American Society of Radiologic Technologists (ASRT), has worked continuously to develop and improve curricula in schools of radiologic technology. The American Registry of Radiologic Technologists (ARRT), sponsored by the American College of Radiology and the ASRT, examines and certifies graduate technologists. Successful candidates earn the title of registered technologist and use the abbreviation R.T. following their names. As the field of radiology continued to expand, the ARRT recognized the need for additional education and certification for radiation therapy and nuclear medicine technologists.

Today there are well over 1,000 AMA-approved schools in the United States. While there is an increasing trend toward two-year associate degree programs in junior colleges and four-year baccalaureate programs, the great majority of schools have hospital-based certificate programs. Although graduates of such schools are fully qualified technologists, the objective of the baccalaureate program is to produce technically competent professionals who are also prepared for administrative and teaching positions. The certificate curriculum requires a minimum of 410 clock hours of didactic instruction in conjunction with a minimum of 2,400 clock hours of clinical instruction. The total length of training must be at least twenty-four months. To qualify for admission one must be a high school graduate with preparation in mathematics and science.

Schools following the curriculum suggested by the ASRT offer courses in the following areas:

X-ray physics
Anatomy and physiology
Principles of radiographic exposure
Darkroom chemistry
Principles of radiation therapy
Orientation to the operating room
Nursing procedures
Standard and special radiographic positioning
Special radiographic procedures
Ethics

Schools that train radiation therapy technologists require that candidates for admission be either graduates of approved schools of radiologic technology or registered nurses who have successfully completed a course in radiation physics. Students who are accepted into these programs spend a minimum of twelve months in training to become eligible to take a registry examination in the specialty of radiation therapy technology. Those who achieve satisfactory scores on the registry examination become registered radiation therapy technologists.

Accredited schools of nuclear medicine technology require that candidates for admission be registered medical laboratory technologists, registered radiologic technologists, registered nurses, or have a baccalaureate degree from an accredited college or university with a major in the biological or physical sciences. Students who are accepted then receive one full year of instruction and clinical experiences in the isotope laboratory. After they successfully complete this work, students are eligible to take the registry examination in nuclear medicine technology, thereby becoming registered nuclear medicine technologists.

Technologists who have earned certification following twenty-four months of training but have no professional work experience earn from $6,000 to $8,500 annually. Technologists with baccalaureate degrees begin at annual salaries ranging from $7,500 to $10,000.

SUMMARY

Approved schools graduate approximately 7,000 students each year, but far greater numbers are needed to supply technologists for the more than 7,000 hospitals, 5,000 clinics, and several thousand laboratories in private offices. Opportunities exist in rural areas as well as in urban centers.

Those considering careers in radiologic technology must have compassion for the sick and injured. Emotional maturity is essential if the technologist is to work effectively in the hospital environment.

BIBLIOGRAPHY

Donizetti, P.: Shadow and substance, New York, 1967, Pergamon Press.

Grigg, E. R. N.: The trail of the invisible light, Springfield, Ill., 1965, Charles C Thomas, Publisher.

Grigg, E. R. N.: The new history of radiology, Radiol. Techn. 36:229, 1965.

Horizons unlimited, ed. 8, Chicago, 1970, American Medical Association.

Roth, C. J., and Weimer, L.: Hospital health services, New York, 1964, Henry Z. Walck, Inc.

The challenge—radiologic technology. The future—yours, New York, 1968, E. R. Squibb & Sons, Inc.

X-rays and you, Rochester, N. Y., 1965, Eastman Kodak Co.

PROFESSIONAL ORGANIZATIONS WHERE FURTHER INFORMATION CAN BE OBTAINED:

American Society of Radiologic Technologists
645 North Michigan Avenue
Chicago, Illinois 60611

American Registry of Radiologic Technologists
2600 Wayzata Boulevard
Minneapolis, Minnesota 55405

Chapter 16

SPEECH AND HEARING SCIENCE

John W. Black

WHAT IS SPEECH AND HEARING SCIENCE?

Speech and hearing science is neither new nor narrow in scope. It deals with the system man uses for verbal communication. Conversation, public speeches, acting, or reading aloud are all means of communicating, whether the parties are face to face or use electronic equipment. It is acoustic, involving talking and listening. These systems are so important that persons with defective speech or hearing are often treated at public expense. Moses lamented, "I am slow of speech," and commonly special reference is made to a person's speech skills. For example, letters of recommendation often include comments on the manner in which a person communicates and refer to the quality of his voice, articulation, pronunciation, and vocabulary. (See Fig. 20.)

Specialists in speech and hearing science may be referred to as speech and hearing therapists, speech pathologists and audiologists, logopedists, or phoniatrists. They have studied such topics as (1) speech and hearing disorders; (2) the development of language; (3) the development of language processes in children; (4) language and speech for the deaf; (5) vocal pitch, loudness, and quality; (6) the physics (acoustics) of speech; (7) the anatomy and physiology of the head and neck and the process of respiration; (8) the theories and measurement of hearing; (9) semantics; and (10) phonetics.

The speech and hearing scientist does not work alone. He is a member of a team whose members vary according to the special needs of each patient or client. Team members may be teachers, medical specialists (pediatricians, surgeons, otologists, neurologists, physiatrists, and psychiatrists), dental specialists, psychologists, nurses, and social workers. The typical specialist in speech and hearing works with other professional people and serves individuals of all ages.

In hospital settings, speech and hearing specialists see patients recovering from laryngectomies or surgical repair of cleft palates.

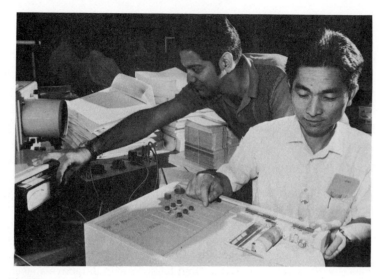

Fig. 20. Speech and hearing scientists are studying the intonation patterns of some well-known speakers for research purposes.

They may also work with those who are considering an operation on the middle ear as well as those who have Parkinson's disease or who have suffered a stroke. In schools they often work with children who talk with obvious misarticulations, stutter, have voice disorders, or a loss of hearing. In clinics, speech and hearing specialists deal with all of these types of disorders in addition to working with persons who seek assistance in learning to communicate more effectively. In industry they may assess the hearing of employees who work in an environment where there are high noise levels. They may work in laboratories to improve hearing aids and telephones or design electronic devices that people can use for self-instruction.

WHAT IS THE HISTORY OF SPEECH AND HEARING SCIENCE?

Speech and hearing science has been the subject of much study. In 1779 the annual prize of the Russian Academy of Science was awarded for an explanation and successful simulation of vowel sounds. Although Alexander Graham Bell is best known for his work on the telephone, this invention evolved from his achievements as a phonetician (a student of speech sounds) and his work in teaching deaf persons to communicate. His interest in the field had been spurred by his wife's acute hearing loss. Sir Richard Paget, an Englishman with interests similar to Bell's, served as President of the British Deaf and Dumb Association and wrote an especially scholarly account of a theory of the origin of language, a work that contrasts sharply with Bell's phonetics books and inventions with their practical applications. Professor Edward Scripture was absorbed with the same core of facts that intrigued Bell and Paget. He worked first as an experimental psychologist and subsequently as a theoretical and practical speech pathologist. Scripture's works related primarily to talking rather than hearing and illustrate the diversity among speech pathologists and audiologists, or speech and hearing scientists. Harvey Fletcher began his career in speech and hearing science as a physicist in a university. His interests expanded in many directions as he coped with the topics of telephony in the Bell Telephone Laboratories. The insights of this distinguished researcher extended the horizons of speech and hearing science. Herman Helmholtz, an eminent German psychologist and physicist, maintained an active interest in hearing. His monumental volume, *The Sensation of Tone,* is available to students of speech and hearing science in a highly readable English translation by the dedicated phonetician Alexander J. Ellis, who studied and translated the epoch-making work of Helmholtz in his own search for a rationale for the perception of speech.

These examples illustrate the many phases of speech and hearing science, or speech pathology and audiology. They may clarify why the term "speech and hearing scientist" is used in this chapter to represent the fully trained practitioner-teacher-researcher, the product of sustained undergraduate, graduate, and professional specialization.

WHAT ARE THE CRITERIA OF ADEQUATE VOICE COMMUNICATION?

From the point of view of speech and hearing science, the following principal criteria are used to evaluate the communication system: (1) intelligibility both in talking and in hearing; (2) pleasantness of voice and minimal distraction in the production of speech; and (3) an adequate vocabulary and use of correct syntax.

Intelligibility can be graded, that is, given a numerical score. Intelligibility depends on the speaker, the listener, the acoustics of the room in which the speaking takes place, and the unit at a person's ear; for example, a telephone receiver or a hearing aid.

Pleasantness in speech is first an absence of certain readily identifiable vocal qualities, rhythms, and patterns of pitch that are identified with speech disorders. Reducing the distracting movements and mannerisms that may accompany abnormal talking has more that just cosmetic value.

The language that is used in talking is evaluated at all ages. Is this child developing normally? Can this patient make sense? Can either one of them understand me? Here the topic is normal versus abnormal speech and language. The professional worker must also be interested in the adequacy of speech skills for special uses. For example, a person who is employing a sales clerk, receptionist, or telephone operator needs people whose speech will be effective in those situations.

WHAT ARE THE NEEDS FOR PROFESSIONAL SPEECH AND HEARING SCIENTISTS?

Because speech and hearing skills affect our public as well as our private lives, the shortage of people who are trained to work with speech and hearing is especially critical. This shortage affects universities, state and local health agencies, and schools, and accordingly there is an increasing use of supportive personnel such as hospital corpsmen trained in audiology who work with speech pathologists and audiologists.

Training programs for supportive personnel are only now being developed. The laws in some states permit agencies to sponsor in-service programs to train high school graduates as audiometrists. Some universities are also experimenting with brief courses of study to train aides who will work routinely with isolated segments of speech therapy.

HOW DOES ONE STUDY SPEECH AND HEARING SCIENCE?

Speech and hearing science may be taught in university or college departments established to deal with these areas, or relevant courses may be offered in a number of departments involved with different subjects related to speech and hearing.

Undergraduate students majoring in speech and hearing science study voice and diction, acoustics, phonetics, speech development in children, anatomy and physiology of the ear and vocal mechanisms, and introductory speech pathology and audiology. They study psychology and should include courses in languages, linguistics, anthropology, mathematics, and biology in their undergraduate programs. This course work constitutes preprofessional study.

It is important that graduate students clearly keep in mind the professional requirements of the American Speech and Hearing Association. To qualify for a certificate of clinical competence, candidates must meet the following requirements:

1. They must be members of the American Speech and Hearing Association.

2. They must submit transcripts from one or more accredited colleges or universities presenting evidence of the completion of a well-integrated program of sixty semester hours that includes eighteen semester hours in the normal development and use of speech, hearing, and language and forty-two semester hours in the management of speech, hearing, and language disorders and in supplementary or related fields. Of these forty-two semester hours, at least six must be in audiology (for the speech pathologist) or in speech pathology (for the audiologist). No more than six may be in courses that provide academic credit for clinical practice. At least twenty-four semester hours, not including credit for a thesis or dissertation, must be in courses in the field in which certification is being sought. Furthermore, thirty semester hours must be in courses that may be applied toward a graduate degree by the college or university at which these courses are taken.

3. They must submit evidence of the completion of 275 clock hours of supervised, direct clinical experience in working with individuals who have a variety of communication disorders. This experience must be obtained within the training institution or in one of its cooperating programs, and more than half of this experience must be obtained during graduate study.

4. They must also present written references from employers and supervisors of nine months of full-time professional employment in the area in which certification is being sought.

5. Finally, candidates must pass a nationally administered written examination.

Simultaneously with their professional study, prospective specialists master the tools of research and independent study to enable them to approach a client in the spirit of inquiry rather than prescription. They read the professional literature with understanding and seek to make their own contributions to it.

Much of the students' practical experience is gained through work in a speech and hearing clinic. Typical university clinics offer four types of interrelated services:

1. They provide opportunities for prospective professionals in public schools, colleges, hospitals, community agencies, private clinics, or private practice to work with and observe clinical cases.
2. They provide clinical cases for original study and research in speech and hearing disorders.
3. They extend free services to university students who have impaired hearing or speech deviations.
4. They render services in speech correction and hearing disorders to members of the general community.

The typical university clinic is coordinated by a director or supervisor. He accepts cases for examination and therapy in keeping with the four purposes of the clinic and according to its best interest. He maintains and preserves a record on each person who is accepted for examination or therapy. Such clinics handle a variety of cases:

1. *Speech:* Each client, upon appointment, is given a speech evaluation and recommendations are made. Most therapy is individual. When there is a sufficient number of persons with a similar defect, supplemental clinics are organized for corrective group instruction. The following types of groups may be formed:
   a. Children 4 to 7 years of age with delayed speech problems
   b. Children 5 to 8 years of age with articulation difficulties
   c. Children who stutter
   d. Children with repaired palates
   e. Stutterers 10 to 16 years of age
   f. Adult stutterers
   g. Patients with brain injuries (aphasics)
   h. Individuals who have undergone laryngectomies
   i. Persons who have foreign accents
   j. Adults with voice problems
2. *Hearing:* The services include audiometric testing, lipreading instruction, auditory training, speech correction for the articulatory and voice disorders that occur in many instances with a loss of hearing, and hearing aid evaluations.

All services are coordinated with those offered by other members of the allied health professions.

Current salary scales for speech pathologists and audiologists relate closely to the different levels of training and are further contingent on regional cost-of-living indices.

Level of training	Median (beginning) salary (first 9 to 10 months)
Doctoral	$12,800
Master	$ 9,200
Bachelor	$ 7,000
Other supportive personnel	4/5 of next higher level

*   *   *

The following case study illustrates the various contributions that speech and hearing scientists can make in evaluating client problems and helping clients to achieve improvements.

Mrs. Burns brought her 7-year-old son Tommy to the University Speech and Hearing Clinic. She stated that Tommy had difficulty in forming "s" sounds, that he was unable to make himself understood, and that he stuttered at times. According to his mother, Tommy's early motor and speech development had been normal. He had just completed the first grade, and he reportedly enjoyed it very much. However, his teacher reported that he confused many words due to his inability to differentiate between many of the sounds in the English language. Because of this difficulty, he will attend summer school five mornings a week, as his teacher felt this additional stimulation and training period would give him better preparation for the second grade. Tommy has a brother Steven who is 5 years of age. The brothers are quite close and usually play harmoniously together, according to their mother.

Mrs. Burns is divorced and works as a clerk in a department store. While she is at work, her mother babysits with the children. When he stays with his grandmother, Tommy does not receive much stimulation even from children's television programs, since he is permitted to watch only his grandmother's favorite programs. For example, he has never seen "Sesame Street" or any of the shows designed especially to interest youngsters.

Mrs. Burns was 30 years of age when Tommy was born. She reported that hemorrhaging had occurred approximately twenty-four hours before his birth, which was two weeks premature. Although Tommy weighed 8 pounds when he was born, he was placed in an incubator for two weeks.

Mrs. Burns appeared to be an interested, intelligent parent. She realized that Tommy could benefit from greater environmental stimulation and was receptive to the examiner's recommendations for improvement in this area.

141

A specialized articulation test was administered and Tommy was found to make the following errors:

1. At the beginning of words he would substitute s for "ch" and say *soo* for "chew"; substitute *w* for "r" and say *wed* for "red"; substitute g for "j," saying *gill* for "jill"; substitute d for "th," saying *dough* for "though"; and substitute d for 'z," saying *dip* for "zip."

2. In the middle of words, Tommy would substitute *k* for "t," saying *kiken* for "kitten"; substitute s for "sh," saying *fasin* for "fashion"; substitute d for "r," saying *tidesome* for "tiresome"; substitute *h* for "th," saying *gaher* for "gather"; and substitute g for "z," saying *regen* for "reason."

3. At the end of some words, Tommy would substitute d for "r," saying *load* for "lower."

When asked to do so, Tommy was successful in pronouncing *sh, t, ch, z,* and *th* in nonsense syllables such as "sha," "ta," "cha," "za," and "tha"; and there did not seem to be anything wrong with his articulatory mechanism. He could move his tongue at will and had intact teeth, palate, and lips. Pure-tone audiometry tests indicated that his hearing was within normal limits. However, when he was asked to repeat words as he heard them, he made more mistakes than would be expected, missing five of the thirteen items on the Boston University Short Discrimination Test. On the Peabody Picture Vocabulary Test, Form B, Tommy attained the raw score of 60, a mental age of 6 years and 10 months, and an I.Q. of 89. On the geometric form copying task, Tommy successfully copied the circle, cross, square, and triangle—a performance level appropriate for a child 6 years of age. On the Goodenough Draw-A-Man Test, Tommy's drawing was characteristic of a child 5 years and 9 months of age.

Tommy is right-handed. His performance in hopping on one foot, throwing a ball, running, and rail walking indicated normal gross motor coordination. His manipulation of the pencil for drawing demonstrated normal fine motor coordination. No dysfluencies were noted during the diagnostic evaluation, nor could they be precipitated by increasing communicative stress.

On the basis of these tests and observations, it was concluded that Tommy had a moderate functional articulation problem and poor auditory discrimination skills. It was therefore recommended that he be enrolled for speech therapy, with special emphasis to be placed on building his auditory awareness in general and his auditory discrimination skill in particular. His progress or improvement was to be measured after three months of therapy through administration of the Peabody Picture Vocabulary Test,

Form A. Mrs. Burns was advised to check the public library for reading material on speech and language acquisition.

The low level of Tommy's environmental stimulation appears to be a strong etiological factor in his general lack of awareness of sounds and existing differences between sounds. Although he is stimulable for many of his error phonemes, prognosis is only fair due to his distinct deficiency in auditory discrimination.

BIBLIOGRAPHY

Davis, H., and Silverman, S. R.: Hearing and deafness, New York, 1960, Holt, Rinehart & Winston, Inc.

Denes, P. B., and Pinson, E. N.: The speech chain, Baltimore, 1963, The Williams & Wilkins Co.

Van Riper, C.: Speech correction: principles and methods, ed. 4, Englewood Cliffs, N. J., 1963, Prentice-Hall, Inc.

Wise, C. M.: Introduction to phonetics, Englewood Cliffs, N. J., 1957, Prentice-Hall, Inc.

PROFESSIONAL ORGANIZATION WHERE FURTHER INFORMATION CAN BE OBTAINED:

American Speech and Hearing Association
9030 Old Georgetown Road
Washington, D. C. 20014

Chapter 17

MEDICAL SOCIAL WORK

Mae M. Davis

Patients who are not overburdened by social, financial, and emotional problems are very often the patients who respond best to medical treatment. A patient who fears the loss of a job requiring maximum physical effort because he has suffered damage to his heart, a mother who frets because she has had to leave her young children while she is confined to a hospital, a diabetic patient who has depended upon restaurants for most of his meals and who must now adhere to a restricted diet, a paraplegic whose family must adjust to her doing household tasks from a wheelchair—whatever the nature of the problem, if it is severe enough to retard recovery and lengthen the period of convalescence, the services of the medical social worker are needed. In cases such as these, this highly trained professional becomes an integral part of the patient's total treatment. (See Fig. 21.)

PROFESSIONAL DEVELOPMENT

By the turn of the century, certain physicians had become increasingly aware that social factors play an important role in the cause and treatment of diseases. This awareness led in part to the establishment of medical social work as a specialty in the field of social work at Massachusetts General Hospital in Boston in 1905. By 1910 the New York School of Social Work, in cooperation with Belleview Hospital in New York City, developed a major course of study for hospital social service workers. The role of the medical social worker evolved from these pioneering efforts in Boston and New York.

In the course of its development the social work profession has used many different approaches in working with the various elements of human society—family, community, and ethnic or racial groups—and with the relationships and institutions involved in man's daily life and well-being. Medical social work has traditionally been concerned with the individual who has been moved from

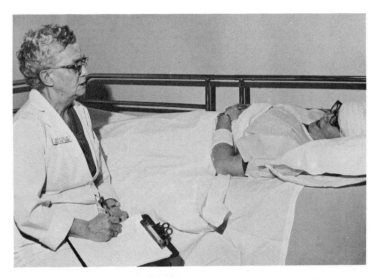

Fig. 21. A young mother, requiring hospitalization following an automobile accident, discusses with a medical social worker the need for community agency care for her small child.

his family setting to the confines of a hospital or institution because of an illness. Through various changes in role, the medical social worker has become actively engaged in helping to extend the concept of medical care beyond the walls of the hospital. Medical social work traditionally dealt only with stresses in the crisis situation of hospitalization. Today it is involved with programming health care to help prevent breakdowns in social function and promote rehabilitation.

EDUCATIONAL REQUIREMENTS

Medical social service departments within hospitals carry out their programs of helping patients through professional standards of practice. In order to maintain these standards, directors of medical social service departments must hold master's degrees in social work. Such departments usually hire staff social workers with master's degrees and assistant social workers who have earned degrees in social welfare from those colleges and universities accredited by the Council on Social Work Education.

Master's and doctor's degrees are awarded for advanced study to students who have demonstrated their abilities in supervisory and leadership roles in a number of practice areas in the field of social work. As of 1969, undergraduate programs in social work or social welfare were offered by more than 200 colleges. The number of schools whose curricula are approved by the Council on Social Work Education is steadily increasing. The bachelor's degree is accepted as the initial certificate for professional practice in social work. As of 1970, graduates of baccalaureate programs in social work are eligible to apply for regular membership in the National Association of Social Workers. Persons with a bachelor's degree in such related fields as sociology, psychology, or education who are currently employed in social work agencies may apply for an associate membership.

Candidates for the baccalaureate degree must meet the college or university's basic requirements for course work in the arts and sciences. Usually students must complete courses in the social sciences, the natural sciences, and the humanities and take courses concerned with the development of basic reading, writing, and verbal communication skills. Typical requirements include a selection of courses in such areas as anthropology, biology, geology, zoology, philosophy, sociology, psychology, history, certain foreign languages, and English. The student majoring in social work follows a course sequence for the first two years that is approved by the department or school of social work.

Curriculum requirements for the junior and senior years consist essentially of courses in social work, sociology, and choices from a specified group of electives. These are typically concentrated in such areas as social systems, social policy, criminology, social factors in personality, race relations, juvenile delinquency, behavior and social movements, sociology or urban life, social welfare and human needs, and government social welfare programs and policies. In their senior year, students are assigned to social agencies, health agencies, hospitals, schools, and other institutions so that they can observe professionals at work and acquire supervised experience. Students who want to specialize in medical social work must earn their bachelor's and master's degrees and complete a period of professionally supervised experience in a hospital or health care facility. In other words, it is not possible to major in medical social work in either graduate or undergraduate social work programs.

PROFESSIONAL FUNCTIONS

Social work as a profession is an art and science concerned with meeting and satisfying human and social needs. It is directed toward serving both individuals and the society in which they live. Social workers achieve their objectives by working with individuals, families, and the community. Medical social workers usually work in situations where individuals are confined to hospitals or are being treated in clinics for illness or injury. The medical social worker employs two primary skills in working with patients: the art of listening and the art of establishing a carefully and consciously developed relationship. Data are gathered for every patient and developed into a medical-social history for the use of physicians and other members of the patient-care team who participate in treatment and planning. Medical social work may involve not only interviews with the patient but also consultation with family members, friends, employers, teachers, and ministers as well as with personnel from other hospitals and health care and social service agencies. It involves referrals to service agencies in the community where various kinds of follow-up help are available to the patient after his discharge from the hospital. Hospital medical social workers may continue to serve a former patient in outpatient clinics and through home visits. Medical social work requires contact with the patient's physician, skill in reading medical chart progress records, and an understanding of medical terminology relating to treatment procedures and medical-surgical diagnoses. At times the medical social worker must interpret a diagnosis and its significance to the patient, his family, and other social workers in the community who may become involved.

The following account, adapted from *Helping The Dying Patient and His Family* by Nathalie Kennedy, illustrates the activities of a medical social worker.

Mrs. S., 30 years of age, a registered nurse and mother of four children, was referred to the caseworker at the time her 3-year-old daughter Cheryl had an eye removed because of a tumor behind the eyeball. The prognosis for Cheryl was poor.

The reason for the referral was that Mrs. S., experiencing conflict about her roles as nurse and mother, had exhibited explosive behavior on the ward. As a nurse she was able to understand the seriousness of her daughter's illness but found it hard to accept because the onset had been so sudden, and because she had considered Cheryl to be the healthiest, brightest, and most outgoing of her four children.

At the outset she resented the referral but the caseworker was able to convince her that the staff was genuinely interested in helping her and recognized that she was upset with good reason.

The worker also pointed out that frequently professional people find it difficult to maintain an objective attitude when they attempt to assist family members with whom they are emotionally involved. She was then able to appraise her actions, to be less critical of the nursing staff, and to turn over the responsibilities for the child's care to them. Her relationship with members of the medical staff also improved.

In the meantime, neighbors in the close-knit community in which the family resided had rallied behind the famly and were helping to care for the children at home, thus enabling their father to resume working as an engineer with an aircraft firm. Mrs. S. was grateful for the assistance but distressed that it was necessary. The worker helped her to see that the neighbors were glad to be helpful and that she should accept the help in the spirit in which it was given.

Mrs. S. became increasingly able to handle her anxieties but was concerned about her husband who, she felt, was having trouble in facing the seriousness of Cheryl's illness. In a lengthy discussion with the caseworker, Mr. S. expressed anger toward the doctors because he felt there had been too long a delay before the surgery was performed. The worker was able to show him that his anger toward the medical staff was related to his own frustration and helplessness in the situation. She suggested that he express his feelings to the chief resident as he was the one who had followed Cheryl through all her hospitalizations, and she arranged such a meeting. She also told him about his wife's concern for him. Mrs. S. later reported that the interview had helped them both and that they were reaching toward each other for needed support and comfort.

Cheryl's condition continued to decline and during the last few days preceding her death, the caseworker talked frequently with the parents, encouraging them to express their feelings and discussing with them how they might best prepare the other children. Both parents took their daughter's death quite well. The caseworker continued counseling Mrs. S. who with her children remained under Medical Center care for several months.

In summary, the worker felt that although Mrs. S. had been initially resistive to the referral, she was able to use the help given, not only in relation to facing Cheryl's illness and death but in relation to other problem areas. She evidenced good ego strength and became able to handle subsequent crisis situations such as a possible neurological disorder in the oldest child which was later ruled out. After eight months, when no further problems had arisen, the case was closed.*

*Adapted from Kennedy, N.: Helping the dying patient and his family, New York, 1960, Family Service Association of America, pp. 123-125.

FURTHER SCOPE OF RESPONSIBILITY

Medical social workers are responsible for keeping adequate records of the services rendered to every patient. They are required to attend various medical and surgical conferences with groups of physicians, nurses, and other health professionals to discuss patient situations and to plan for the best follow-up patient care. Their responsibilities may also involve budget and financial assistance planning with patients and their families to ensure their having adequate housing, medicines, equipment such as a wheelchair and hospital bed, transportation to and from the clinic or doctor's office, and adequate food and clothing.

CAREER OPPORTUNITIES

This has been only a brief overview of the many services rendered by the medical social worker in a hospital. It should be remembered that these professionals also perform their services in various health agencies, welfare departments, extended care facilities, nursing homes, and other patient care institutions.

There are numerous professional opportunities in medical social work, and indeed in all fields of social work, both in government and in private settings. Approximately 175,000 job openings in 1970 were predicted from 1965 studies made by the United States Department of Labor. There are many opportunities available in specialized areas such as psychiatric programs for the mentally ill or mentally retarded, children's and family services, adoption services, mental health programs, rehabilitation, government welfare programs, and services to the aged, blind, crippled, and disabled. Many volunteer organizations such as the Epilepsy Association, American Cancer Society, American Heart Association, the Kidney Foundation, the Arthritis Foundation, and their state and local auxiliary organizations also employ medical social workers.

The National Association of Social Workers, Inc., through its Committee on Professional Standards and Practice, has established salary standards that are based on the social worker's academic training and experience. Beginning salaries for social workers with bachelor's degrees range from $6,000 to $9,000 annually, and they compare favorably with beginning salaries offered to persons entering other professional fields such as teaching. The salary range for beginning medical social workers with master's degrees extends from $8,000 to $9,500 annually.

SUMMARY

Medical social workers are experts in the field of human relations, trained to understand people and their needs. They use their knowledge, skills, and judgment to help the patient and his family handle their social, emotional, and financial problems. In addition, they must have a thorough knowledge of the community resources that are available to aid the troubled patient and his family. The medical social worker needs objectivity and good judgment in order to view all angles of human problems with warm and compassionate understanding from a practical and realistic perspective.

BIBLIOGRAPHY

Baker, R. L., and Briggs, T. L.: Differential use of social work manpower, New York, 1968, National Association of Social Workers, Inc.

Perlman, H. H.: Persona-social role and personality, Chicago, 1968, The University of Chicago Press.

Perlman, H. H., editor: Helping—Charlotte Towle on social work and social casework, Chicago, 1969, The University of Chicago Press.

PROFESSIONAL ORGANIZATIONS WHERE FURTHER INFORMATION CAN BE OBTAINED:

National Association of Social Workers, Inc.
2 Park Avenue
New York, New York 10016

Council on Social Work Education
345 East 46th Street
New York, New York 10017

National Commission for Social Work Careers
345 East 46th Street
New York, New York 10017

Chapter 18

HOSPITAL AND HEALTH SERVICES ADMINISTRATION

Barbara McCool

The health care administrator has the responsibility of managing the complex organization of the modern hospital or health facility. The administrator's role is to provide quality patient care efficiently through the combined efforts of all members of the health care team.

The health care administrator is directly responsible to a board of trustees, a group of civic-minded community leaders who determine broad policies and objectives. The administrator directs the day-to-day activities of the institution and assumes a major role in planning and promoting the development of health care services. In larger institutions this may involve supervising and coordinating the activities of more than thirty highly specialized departments that perform administrative, professional, or maintenance and operational services.

Health care administrators act to ensure that the health care facility operates efficiently as a unit; they see that necessary facilities, equipment, and services are available; they help coordinate the development of educational programs for nurses, physicians, technologists, and other personnel; and they oversee the facility's contributions to preventive medicine and to improving the health of the people the facility serves. Besides providing the optimum internal environment, the administrator represents the hospital in the community, in the state through representation in the state hospital association, and nationally through participation in the work of the American Hospital Association, American College of Hospital Administrators, and the American Public Health Association.

HISTORY OF THE PROFESSION

Hospital and health services administration emerged as a profession during the 1930s with the formation of the American College of Hospital Administrators. The American College of Hospital

Administrators, acting as a professional organization, established standards of competence and education for hospital administrators and standards for research in hospital administration. Through the influence of this professional organization, graduate programs in hospital administration grew.

The field of hospital and health services administration was developed to meet the changing health needs of society. At the turn of the century, hospitals were places for people with terminal illnesses, and the hospital superintendent's primary job was to act as the custodian of property and equipment. However, since the 1930s, when social change began to sweep through hospitals, the administrator's job has become more specialized and complex.

Health care administrators are now responsible for the management of community hospitals, large medical teaching centers, neighborhood health centers, public health organizations, planning and financing agencies, regional medical programs, and extended care facilities. Many of these institutions are multimillion dollar operations that employ thousands of people.

EDUCATIONAL PREPARATION

Preparation for a career in hospital and health services administration begins in college with a liberal arts or business administration degree. After earning a bachelor's degree, the student pursues graduate work at the master's level.

The curriculum of a program in hospital and health care administration provides both academic study and work experience. Students may earn master's degrees in hospital administration, business administration, or public administration with a specialty in hospital and health care administration. The course of study is organized to introduce the student to hospital and health care administration as soon as possible after he enters the program. Therefore concomitant courses in organization theory and the social and behavioral sciences are taught together with courses pertaining to health care delivery and the management of hospital and health care resources.

Required courses in hospital and health services administration include studies in the following areas:

Hospitals and medical care administration
Environment and structural components of medical care
Foundations of hospital management
Health care system
Functional aspects of hospital management
Hospitals and the community

Dynamics of health services administration
Individual studies in health care administration

Students may also select courses from such subject areas as the following:

Social, economic, and political aspects of medical care
Administrative theory
Health and human behavior
Hospital and health facilities planning
Health economics and financing
Urban, rural, and regional health planning
Labor economics
Communication theory
Public health organization
Biometrics
Community health
Epidemiology and public health
Special problems in medical sociology
Quantitative methods in administration
Systems analysis
Principles of automatic data processing

There are thirty-four graduate programs in hospital and health care administration in the United States. Graduates of these programs hold responsible administrative positions in hospitals, long-term care facilities, governmental and voluntary health agencies, organizations involved in planning for health care delivery, and voluntary and governmental health care financing agencies.

Hospital and health care administrators work closely with physicians, professional and nonprofessional allied health personnel, business and technical personnel, community leaders, university and other hospital administrators, health and city planners, state and national government officials, and patients from all walks of life.

PERSONAL QUALITIES NEEDED

A future health care administrator should possess (1) a commitment to serving others, (2) above-average intelligence, (3) an ability to get along with many different kinds of people, (4) the ability to work under pressure, and (5) adequate physical and emotional stamina.

RELATED PROFESSIONALS

A wide variety of health care professionals are responsible to the health care administrator. Included in this group are assistant administrators who manage different areas and activities of the institution; a comptroller who advises on financial management; a personnel director responsible for hiring staff members and administering the personnel policy; and a public relations director involved with maintaining internal communications and relations with the community and general public. There may also be as many as thirty department heads responsible for the supervision of their areas of specialization in medicine and related fields, such as nursing, physical therapy, and medical records.

*   *   *

The following case study portrays the many responsibilities of a hospital administrator. Mr. Richard Cramer is the administrator of Northfield Community Hospital, a 400-bed, general acute institution operated by a nonprofit corporation in a midwestern city with a population of 500,000. It offers medical, surgical, pediatric, obstetrical, and psychiatric care programs, has modern diagnostic and therapeutic facilities, and cooperates with other hospitals in the area in operating a comprehensive outpatient clinic. It is fully accredited by the Joint Commission on Accreditation of Hospitals and sponsors several medical and allied health educational programs. Mr. Cramer has been the administrator of Northfield for three years. He is active in the American College of Hospital Administrators, serves as a delegate to the American Hospital Association, and is President of the State Hospital Association. He has three assistant administrators, all of whom are active in the civic life of the community.

8:00   Mr. Cramer arrives at the hospital parking lot and is stopped by Dr. Kenneth Stone, Chief of the Medical Staff. Dr. Stone arranges a meeting with Mr. Cramer for 1:30 that afternoon to review the applications of physicians who have applied for medical staff privileges.

8:15   As he approaches the entrance to the hospital, Mr. Cramer meets Mrs. Evans, a member of the hospital's Board of Trustees. Mr. Evans is currently a patient at Northfield, and Mr. Cramer is pleased to learn that Mr. Evans is recuperating from his surgery and will be going home in a few days.

8:25   When Mr. Cramer arrives at his office, his secretary, Miss Rolfe, hands him his appointment schedule for the day, a folder of correspondence, and a list of several phone calls that must be returned. Mr. Cramer glances quickly through his mail, which includes a letter from the Blue Cross Association concerning a revised reimbursement schedule, several thank you notes from patients who have been discharged from the hospital, a letter from the hospital's attorney explaining the institution's legal position in a pending liability case, bids from contractors for construction of a new facility, a letter of resignation from a department head, and confirmation of his reservation for the upcoming annual meeting of the American College of Hospital Administrators.

8:30 Mr. Cramer's three assistants and the Director of Nursing Services arrive for their daily meeting. Mrs. Smiley presents the patient census for the day, reports on happenings on the night shift, and on the condition of critical patients. Mr. Pace distributes copies of the pharmacy reorganization plans that will be presented at the meeting of department heads later in the day. He also announces that he will be representing the hospital at a planning meeting for the coronary care educational program to be sponsored by the state's regional medical program. Mr. Brooks reports that the parking lot construction will be slowed down by a delay in the delivery of entrance gates and that representatives of the housekeeping employees' union have approached him about negotiations for a new union contract. Mr. Parks reports that he and Dr. Summerfield will be leaving the next day to recruit interns and residents for the following year. Mr. Cramer announces that the revised wage and salary program will be discussed at an administration meeting to be held the following day, when a decision will be made about implementation. He also reports that he has been successful in hiring a public relations director to handle all hospital communications. During a discussion of plans for a new coronary unit, the hospital's architect arrives with drawings to be submitted to the Board of Trustees for approval. During the meeting, Miss Rolfe is busy answering telephone calls and arranging appointments. The meeting ends abruptly as the administrator is summoned to the emrgency room, where the town's mayor has just been brought in following an automobile accident. Mr. Cramer instructs Miss Rolfe concerning notification of the press.

10:00 The President of the Board of Trustees arrives to discuss the agenda for the Board meeting to be held that evening.

11:30 Mr. Cramer addresses a luncheon meeting of the Kiwanis Club on the cost of medical care.

1:30 Dr. Stone arrives to review applications for medical staff privileges. The physician wants Mr. Cramer's recommenda-

Fig. 22. Hospital administrators play a crucial role in developing plans for expanded facilities to meet community health needs.

tions prior to a meeting of the Credentials Committee that is scheduled for the following week. A problem that has arisen in the Anesthesiology Department is discussed and resolved.

2:00 Mr. Cramer meets with the Executive Committee of the Southside Health Planning Council about allocation of hospital beds in city-wide medical emergencies.

3:00 Mr. Cramer attends the meeting of department heads and gives a report on the new management training program.

4:00 In a meeting with the hospital Comptroller, the Director of Nursing, and the Personnel Director, Mr. Cramer discusses the Nursing Service budget.

6:00 Mr. Cramer attends a dinner meeting of the Executive Committee of the Board of Trustees and discusses long-range development plans to be presented later at a meeting of the full Board. (See Fig. 22.)

10:00 Following the Executive Committee meeting, Mr. Cramer returns briefly to the hospital to check on the mayor's condition. He is relieved to find him resting comfortably and to learn that his injuries are not serious.

NEED FOR HOSPITAL ADMINISTRATORS

The rapidly expanding demand for comprehensive health care has intensified the need for competent hospital and health care administrators. This has become one of the critical issues facing the American health care system today, and the shortage of administrators will become more severe with the increased emphasis on extended care facilities, community mental health centers, expanded general hospitals, and area-wide planning agencies. Newly graduated hospital administrators may earn from $10,000 to $12,000 annually. Depending upon the size of the facility and the administrator's experience and competence, he may eventually earn from $25,000 to $30,000 a year.

SUMMARY

Today's health care administrators manage complex environments that provide comprehensive health care to patients. The graduate preparation of the administrators focuses on the development of management skills that can be practiced in the health care setting, as the administrator assumes responsibility for coordinating the resources, manpower, and medical programs necessary to provide quality patient care.

BIBLIOGRAPHY

Employment outlook for hospital administrators, Washington, D. C., 1966, Bureau of Labor Statistics, United States Department of Labor.

Health careers guidebook, Washington, D. C., 1965, United States Department of Labor.

Horizons unlimited, ed. 8, Chicago, 1970, American Medical Association.

Hospital administration as a career, Chicago, 1968, American College of Hospital Administrators.

Hospital Management, published monthly by Hospital Management, Inc.

Hospital Progress, published monthly by the Catholic Hospital Association.

Roth, C. J., and Weiner, L.: Hospital health services, New York, 1964, Henry Z. Walck, Inc.

The hospital administrator, Washington, D. C., 1969, Association of University Programs in Hospital Administration.

The Modern Hospital, published monthly by the American Hospital Association.

PROFESSIONAL ORGANIZATIONS WHERE FURTHER INFORMATION CAN BE OBTAINED:

American College of Hospital Administrators
840 North Lake Shore Drive
Chicago, Illinois 60611

The Association of University Programs in Hospital Administration
#1 Dupont Circle
Suite 420
Washington, D. C. 20036

Chapter 19

MEDICAL COMMUNICATIONS

Kathryn Schoen

The communication problems that have developed as a result of the population, information, and technological explosions have encouraged the growth of a new health-related profession, medical communications. This field, a product of rapidly expanding societal needs, brings together a number of the arts and sciences in a new relationship.

The effective dissemination of health information is a basic prerequisite for controlling disease. Scientists need current research information, teachers need better ways of transmitting the increasing volume of knowledge to larger numbers of students, practicing health professionals need to keep abreast of advances in medicine, and consumers of health services need to know what services are available and where and how they may be secured.

These messages may be simple or complex; the intended audiences range from the least sophisticated to those already highly knowledgeable. Man's technological skills in transmitting information far exceed his ability to supply the necessary professional manpower and his ability to capitalize on the most effective communications available.

Health professionals, concerned about the time lag (which is primarily a communications gap) between research discoveries and their application to patient needs, are searching for ways to solve this dilemma. There are professionals in the health sciences, there are medical artists and medical photographers, there are radio, television, and audiovisual specialists, there are experts in communications theory, there are scientific writers and medical librarians, there are computer programmers and information science specialists, and there are educators in learning resources and instructional aids. Nonetheless, it is extremely difficult to find personnel trained in communications in its broadest sense who also know the language and environment of the health professions. It has therefore become necessary to develop programs that prepare

Fig. 23. A medical dietetics student interviews a patient to secure a dietary history; medical communication personnel record the interview for student evaluation and improvement of interview skills.

professionals who are expert in medical communications. (See Fig. 23.)

HISTORICAL DEVELOPMENT

Those working in the medical environment have long been concerned with the communication process. Much communication has been chiefly verbal, but there has also been much involvement with the visual media. Before the advent of many technological advances in visual communication, artists were the primary graphic interpreters of ideas and knowledge in medical education. The invention of television and the many improvements in photographic techniques have given considerable impetus to the development of more effective communication processes in the medical environment.

Since television was first introduced into health care facilities in the 1940s, it has been used experimentally in a variety of ways for the purpose of identifying its potential contributions to the medical curriculum. In fact, all types of visual communications tools—books, drawings, models, specimens, exhibits, slides (including stereo), films, programmed instructions, television, lantern slides, audio tapes, computers, and the overhead projector have contributed to advances in medical education as well as in hospital services. Much of the equipment was complex and costly, and when its adaptation to communication needs became critical, it became necessary for all concerned professionals to share ideas regarding its use. As early as 1953 the Audiovisual Conference of Medical and Allied Sciences was organized to further audiovisual education. Much attention was devoted to these channels of communication, but they by no means fulfilled all the communication needs in the health environment.

The first educational programs in medical communications, established in the 1960s, were often referred to as biomedical communication programs. The students were generally drawn from professional schools or doctoral programs, and limited kinds of communications methods were utilized. These programs focused primarily on the technological rather than on the social and behavioral aspects of communication. A program of this type was initiated by the National Medical Audiovisual Center in cooperation with Tulane and other universities.

For some time the National Library of Medicine has supported educational programs that prepare specialists in the automated document- and information-handling networks that have been designed to improve the flow of biomedical information. It has refined its MEDLARS (Medical Literature Analysis and Retrieval System) services to provide many useful bibliographies as well as personnel capable of functioning in this communication system.

EDUCATIONAL PROGRAM

The first attempt to develop a broad communications program for the health areas at an undergraduate level was made at The Ohio State University in 1969, and the course of study has much in common with the basic educational approach used in other baccalaureate degree programs in allied health areas. The medical communications curriculum is a four-year baccalaureate program of study. Prospective medical communicators spend their first two years meeting basic university requirements in the liberal arts and developing an interdisciplinary approach to communication theory and skills. The course sequence crosses departmental lines to provide the student with maximum exposure to the disciplines that are related to medical communications. These include such areas as television and radio production, communication theories and models, sociology, anatomy, biology, photography, and economics.

With this basic foundation, third-year medical communications students focus more on the medical milieu. They learn the language and "feel" of the health environment and delve deeper into the science of communications. In the fourth year the emphasis of each student's program is determined by his area of interest, and he is given the opportunity to conduct medically oriented pilot studies in communications. These studies may investigate such areas as patient and health personnel relationships. They may deal with communication problems in teaching, or they may seek the answers to problems in the readability and intelligibility of medical language. Expanded opportunities are planned for using media equipment and preparing software such as slides, films, and charts. While they involve themselves in actual communications experiences and in communication research projects, fourth-year students learn to select the media or means of communication most appropriate for their own designs. The selection and use of tools for a particular educational objective becomes an immediate challenge.

Medical communications majors need not terminate their formal education at the undergraduate level. Graduate study will allow students to focus more sharply on a specific area and move from the role of generalist to specialist. Some students may choose medical communications research. Some may pursue programs that will assist them in instructional skills or in developing curricula for undergraduate programs. Others may choose to develop management skills to coordinate learning resource centers in health care environments.

MEDICAL COMMUNICATIONS SPECIALISTS

Graduates of baccalaureate programs are generalists—eclectics who use aspects of many specialties to coordinate and improve communications and instruction. They learn to evaluate and then select those communication skills and techniques that will be most effective in meeting each communication need. Medical communicators function as coordinators of educational resources by combining their understanding of the educational and communication processes with a working knowledge of the properties, limitations, and capabilities of available media in their various applications.

Graduates of baccalaureate programs may serve as consultants for continuing education as well as for academic programs in the health professions. They may assist health agencies, professional organizations, and academicians to communicate with either lay or professional audiences. They may participate in the design and implementation of communication research in the medical environment and assist in the planning and development of instructional aids that involve the artistry of the graphic arts or the scientific technology used in computer-assisted instruction. They may work

161

in publishing or public relations. Medical communications specialists continually evaluate all communication efforts in order to improve their effectiveness. They are professionals able to conceptualize as well as act in their attempts to coordinate health needs, communication principles, media, and people.

CONTRIBUTING PROFESSIONALS

Since communications is such a broad area, it draws on the expertise of many disciplines. Medical illustration is one of the areas that contributes to the process of preparing specialists in medical communications. Whether they are using graphic arts for publication, exhibits, or teaching aids, medical illustrators must be versatile and exacting in their contributions to medical communications. They are often required to create software for use with highly sophisticated educational tools—motion pictures, television productions, programmed-learning materials, and other media.

New techniques, systems, and equipment for processing, storing, retrieving, and distributing data have been developed to handle the ever-increasing volume of knowledge and information in the health science field. However, these have not been able to meet the massive demands made by rapid growth. Medical librarians have become responsible for the coordination and dissemination of health science information through the medical communications complex of modern medical centers. Science information specialists develop controls and systems for information flow. A system is an arrangement in which everything is related to everything else, so that a malfunction of any one part affects the work of the entire system. Educational applications of systems concepts are critical. Since students can learn concepts and problem-solving techniques by working with a programmed computer system, these science information specialists and professionals in related fields contribute to the educational preparation of medical communicators.

The broad area of audiovisuals involves many professional and technical personnel, ranging from program developers and writers to production experts. They acquaint medical communications specialists with various audio aids such as taped recordings and help them to understand single-concept teaching devices such as the automatic projectors available for individual student use in library carrels. They produce the television programs that personalize, magnify, multiply, and transport the images that make it possible to bring the clinical setting into the classroom.

The contributions of those who specialize in oral and written communication, whether as theorists or as practitioners, cannot be underestimated. The myriad publications on the market are indicative of the keen competition for control of information dissemination. It is also apparent that there is an insufficient number of people who are qualified to cope with the communications problems in health care settings. Medical communicators attempt to recognize the relationship and mutual dependence that exist among the various professionals who collaborate to produce excellent works using all available methods to achieve superior communication in the health field.

* * *

The following case study illustrates some aspects of the work of specialists in medical communications.

Mrs. Sally Roberts, 37 years of age, is a housewife and the mother of three children, ages 7, 10, and 14 years. She is preparing to leave the hospital after several weeks of treatment and rehabilitation following a stroke that has confined her to a wheelchair. Although she has made excellent progress and has been most anxious to return to her home and family, she has developed many fears and misgivings about the adjustments both she and her family will be forced to make after she leaves the hospital.

Mrs. Roberts had become quite distraught and had spoken at length about her concern with Carol Naylor, a physical therapist and one of the rehabilitation staff members who has been working with her. Miss Naylor discussed the situation with a physiatrist, Dr. Charles Friend, who agreed with the therapist that perhaps they have not been meeting the needs of such patients because of a lack of communication. Dr. Friend suggested that they request the help of someone in medical communications and contacted the director of this department. After the director met with Dr. Friend and Miss Naylor, he agreed that this problem was a legitimate concern of the Medical Communications Center. Helen Richards, a senior student acquiring experience in various areas of medical communications, was assigned to explore this problem. As Mrs. Roberts leaves the hospital, Miss Naylor is able to assure her that help for her and others with similar problems in home adjustment will be forthcoming.

Dr. Friend and Miss Naylor begin to meet with Miss Richards. They describe the communication needs of stroke patients after they return home, and Miss Richards begins to probe for specific data. She asks what information the patients need, at what stages and in what order, what health team members are responsible for instructing patients, what content and procedures seem to need reinforcement for patient retention, which problems seem to be particularly sensitive areas for discussion, and how various patients react. She asks about the various stroke patients' ages, educational backgrounds, interests, number of strokes, and their knowledge of stroke care. She inquires about the amount of treatment patients receive after they return home and from whom they receive it. As the questioning and discussion continue, the exchange is tape recorded for future reference. Miss Richards makes arrangements to visit the rehabilitation center again to collect more data on this problem. She also requests copies of all printed information given to stroke patients.

At the end of a week, Miss Richards has assembled all the applicable stroke-related information she can obtain from the learning resources center, the medical librarian, the regional medical program, the center for continuing medical education, the hospital's own Medical Communications Center, and pertinent professional agencies. She has arranged for a review of a single-concept film that can be used on one of the hospital's teaching machines to judge whether it might help the stroke patient waiting to see a therapist or physician. Dr. Friend and Miss Naylor are also asked to react to several pamphlets Miss Richards has located and to identify information gaps. The possibility of preparing an audio tape that patients can borrow for home use is also discussed.

Within a month of the initial meeting, the following projects are underway:

1. Literature that patients can take home is being prepared, with special attention to readability levels.
2. A lending library of audio tapes is being established for the use of certain patients during their first month at home.
3. A log is prepared so that patients who are receiving therapy can view stroke-related films on certain channels at specific times.
4. A teaching machine with a single-concept film is made available for patients' review while they wait to see their physician or therapist.
5. A method is being developed in cooperation with medical education evaluation specialists so that all channels of communication can be evaluated in the course of medical interviews.

Miss Richards plans to compile a summary of these efforts that Dr. Friend and Miss Naylor can use in teaching medical communications students.

This case study has described only one of the many ways in which medical communications specialists contribute to the health care team.

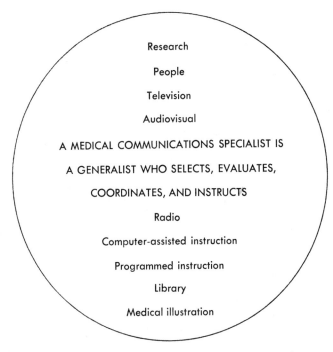

Research

People

Television

Audiovisual

A MEDICAL COMMUNICATIONS SPECIALIST IS

A GENERALIST WHO SELECTS, EVALUATES,

COORDINATES, AND INSTRUCTS

Radio

Computer-assisted instruction

Programmed instruction

Library

Medical illustration

Fig. 24. The role of medical communications specialists.

SUMMARY

Medical communications specialists are experts in learning resources who combine an understanding of communications with a background in medicines, using contributions from the areas depicted in Fig. 24. Medical communications, fresh on the professional scene, answers the need for specialists in communication theory and medical problems. Medical communications specialists disseminate information to improve the quality of patient care, evaluate and enhance techniques in medical and allied health education, and facilitate the processes of communication in all areas of health care.

BIBLIOGRAPHY

Getty, R., editor: Audiovisual conference of medical and allied sciences, Selected Papers from the Fifteenth Annual Meeting, Chicago, 1967.

National Medical Audiovisual Center: Toward improved learning, a collection of significant reprints for the medical educator, Atlanta, no date, Department of Health, Education, and Welfare, United States Public Health Serv-

165

ice, Bureau of Disease Prevention and Environmental Control, National Communicable Disease Center.

Schoen, K.: Proposal for the establishment of a medical communications division within the School of Allied Medical Professions of the College of Medicine, The Ohio State University, Columbus, 1968, unpublished.

Chapter 20

MEDICAL ILLUSTRATION

Mitzi Prosser and James R. Kreutzfeld

Medical illustrators are health professionals who graphically record medical conditions, anatomical and research data, and surgical procedures. They are important members of the medical communications team and work with physicians, research scientists, educators, authors, and many others to record visually the rapidly expanding body of knowledge resulting from modern medical progress. Their artistic talent must be combined with accuracy, attention to minute details, and technical versatility, and they must constantly bear in mind the specific purpose of their work.

HISTORY OF MEDICAL ILLUSTRATION

Medical illustration is a highly specialized profession in which the artist is trained in art and educated in the sciences. Medical illustration is as old as man himself, as evidenced by the primitive anatomical drawings done during the Stone Age on the walls of cave dwellings. Interestingly enough, man's first attempts at illustration depict biological subjects.

Leonardo da Vinci (1442-1519) made a lasting contribution to the science of anatomy. He combined artistic talent, curiosity, and acute observation to produce remarkable sketches that are still used as teaching aids to promote the advancement of medical science.

During the 1500s there were four factors that influenced the growth of medical illustration. Woodblock carving was developed early in this period to help meet the demand for multiple copies of graphic art as well as written material. This led to the production of books, the first teaching machines known to man. Raffaello Santi's accurate depiction of the human body leads us to believe his sketches were based upon the direct observation, dissection, and investigation of cadavers. Jan Stephan Kalkar illustrated the anatomical works of Andreas Vesalius. Together they used woodcuts to produce the anatomical atlases *De Humani Corporis Fabrica*.

From the expanded use of woodcuts to the development of copper engraving, the variety of visual aids in educating people was increasing. The introduction of the printing press, the invention of the process of lithography, and advances in photographic technique opened the way to more efficient methods of producing finished material. These processes were less expensive and required less time. The artists of the late eighteenth century were obviously influential in developing new and better methods for the reproduction of printed and especially of graphic materials.

The early twentieth century saw the establishment of teaching centers where students could acquire the knowledge and skills necessary for a career in medical illustration. A leader in this area was Max Brödel (1870-1946), the man who has had perhaps the greatest influence in the field of medical illustration. Brödel established the first school of medical illustration at The John Hopkins University in 1910. Among his many contributions was his collaboration with Dr. Howard Kelly to produce vital visual materials. He still remains the preeminent figure in medical illustration and has come to be known as the father of medical art.

EDUCATIONAL REQUIREMENTS

Students interested in medical illustration may choose one of several methods of acquiring training for this allied health profession. There are variations in entrance requirements as well as in professional curricula. Some schools offer baccalaureate programs, while others offer programs leading to a graduate degree. Regardless of the entrance requirements, students of medical illustration learn to adapt their artistic skills to the requirements of medical communications, acquiring at the same time a thorough background in the biological sciences. Most programs offer basically the same curriculum but may identify courses by different names.

The following paragraphs describe a program in medical illustration. Students are admitted to the professional curriculum after they have spent two years in an undergraduate program completing the basic requirements of the college or university and the fine arts department. Students are encouraged to visit the department during their freshman and sophomore years and consult with the faculty in planning their course of study.

At the end of their sophomore year, applicants are asked to present a letter describing their interest in medical illustration and a portfolio of their work. A faculty committee reviews this material

Fig. 25. The medical illustration student studies a model of the anatomical structure of the heart as the instructor guides her in sketching techniques.

and selects students to be admitted on the basis of academic qualifications and artistic ability.

Students spend the next two years in the medical illustration program. Practice in executing charts and graphs and in the use of pen and ink, wash, water color, and the airbrush not only develops their skill in using such techniques but also develops their powers of observation. Students are required to take several anatomy courses that cover such areas as (1) fundamental principles of human anatomy supplemented by demonstrations of human material, (2) neuromuscular anatomy of the human body, (3) general histology, a detailed study of the tissues of vertebrate animals, and a general survey of the microscopic structures of various organs, and (4) individual studies of the thorax and abdomen. (See Fig. 25.) In addition, they take photography courses covering (1) basic fundamentals of photography, (2) advanced techniques related to specific topics, with emphasis on creative photography, (3) motion picture production for the theater, television, and the classroom, and (4) special problems in medical photography.

PROFESSIONAL MEDICAL ILLUSTRATION

Medical illustrators may receive assignments from a physician, researcher, or educator in the field of medicine. For example, the surgeon may need a series of sketches done during a particular operation. He calls upon the medical illustrator and together they

169

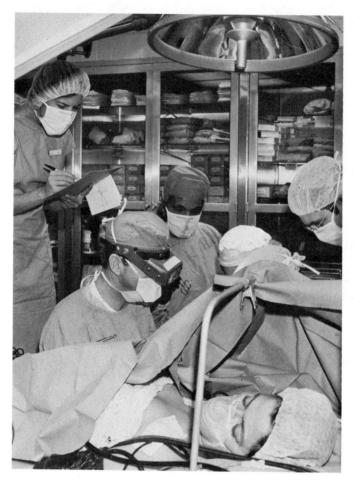

Fig. 26. Preliminary sketching of surgical procedures will result in a finished illustration to be included in a forthcoming textbook.

review the operation before the scheduled surgery. During the operative procedure the medical illustrator may make sketches, take photographs, or both. (See Fig. 26.) Medical illustrators use such sketches or photographs in conjunction with previously published material and further consultation with the surgeon in preparing the actual illustrations. Educational programs in medical illustration prepare students to execute finished illustrations of pertinent surgical, anatomical, and pathological aspects for use in medical textbooks, journals, and other sources. These teaching aids are not only used for the education of medical students, interns, residents, attending staff, and allied health professionals but may be used directly to educate the patient in his own health care needs. Cartooning, animation, exhibit building, and other general art work are also important elements in the education of a medical illustrator.

CAREER OPPORTUNITIES

Medical illustrators work in large teaching universities, medical or research hospitals and centers, scientific institutions, museums, pharmaceutical houses, publishing firms, and commercial art studios, or they may do free-lance work for any of these agencies or for private physicians.

It is important to note when looking for employment that there is a greater need for medical illustrators in the more heavily populated areas around the country. The beginning salaries in the field range from $6,500 to $8,500 annually, depending upon the abilities and responsibilities of the illustrator and upon the needs of the employer.

If medical illustrators wish to pursue their education at the graduate level, there are programs available that offer the opportunity to structure an interdisciplinary approach to an illustrator's specific areas of interest. Such a program may broaden concepts and strengthen skills in teaching, administration, communication, and research.

SUMMARY

Professional medical illustrators prepare visual material for scientific education, whether it is for publication, exhibits, or teaching aids such as slides, movies, or television. The work requires that they be exact yet versatile in each of the communication media. Medical illustrators use a wide variety of visual media such as drawing, painting, sculpture, and photography, and their illustrations may be either realistic or diagrammatic. Some illustrators specialize in one medium; others use several. Sometimes illustrators concentrate on work within one of the medical specialties such as ophthalmology, surgery, or pediatrics. Medical illustrators play an important role in educating the entire community as well as members of the health professions.

BIBLIOGRAPHY

Bethke, E. G.: Basic drawing for biology students, Springfield, Ill., 1969, Charles C Thomas, Publisher.

Clarke, C. D.: Illustration—its technique and application to the sciences, Baltimore, 1939, John D. Lucas Co., Publishers.

McLarty, M. C.: Illustrating medicine and surgery, Baltimore, 1960, The Williams & Wilkins Co.

Price, F.: Medical illustration (do-it-yourself basis), Proc. Roy. Soc. Med. **62**:815, 1969.

Waters, L. B.: The mechanics of medical and dental visualization, Springfield, Ill., 1963, Charles C Thomas, Publisher.

Zollinger, R. M., and Howe, C. T.: The illustration of medical lectures, London, 1964, British Medical Association, vol. 14 (No. 3).

Zollinger, R. M., Pace, W., and Kienzle, G. J.: A practical outline for preparing medical talks and papers, New York, 1961, The Macmillan Co.

PROFESSIONAL ORGANIZATION WHERE FURTHER INFORMATION CAN BE OBTAINED:

Association of Medical Illustrators
c/o Octavia Garlington
Medical Art Services
Medical College of Georgia
Augusta, Georgia 30902

Chapter 21

ENVIRONMENTAL SANITATION

Jack B. Hatlen

Sanitarians are so closely involved with health problems relating to man's environment that these health professionals are frequently referred to as environmental sanitarians. They work to reduce or prevent the spread of many communicable diseases by controlling and manipulating the environment. In order to achieve this goal, environmental sanitarians must work closely with many other allied health professionals as well as with the general public.

HISTORICAL DEVELOPMENT

The major epidemics of such diseases as typhoid, diphtheria, and dysentery that have occurred over the years were spread from man to man and by components of our environment that we need for our daily existence such as food, milk, and water. These components have become contaminated through the actions of man himself. Other diseases such as typhus, plague, yellow fever, and malaria are transmitted to man by infected insects and rodents that share and are a part of our environment. These potential vectors of disease can be controlled by improving man's general environment.

In recent years, environmental sanitarians have become involved with more than just disease prevention. They spend more time today on efforts to improve the environment so that people may work more efficiently and enjoy life more fully. In this respect, environmental sanitarians work to establish environmental control programs relating to water, air, land use, and industrial hygiene. They work in a variety of institutions, including hospitals, convalescent centers, nursing homes, and schools. This change of emphasis and activity indicates that the prevention of communicable disease has become less a problem and concern, and it reflects practices that can enhance the already high standard of living that is enjoyed generally in the United States. In many parts of the world, however, disease control through sanitation practices requires a major effort and has first priority for environmental control specialists.

WHAT DOES THE ENVIRONMENTAL SANITARIAN DO?

As a first step in accomplishing "environmental control," sanitarians conduct inspections or surveys to determine what environmental conditions exist that may be detrimental to our well-being. After a review of these findings they outline those procedures or practices necessary to eliminate the potentially harmful or hazardous conditions. Education—informing people of needed changes, why they are necessary, and how they can be made—is

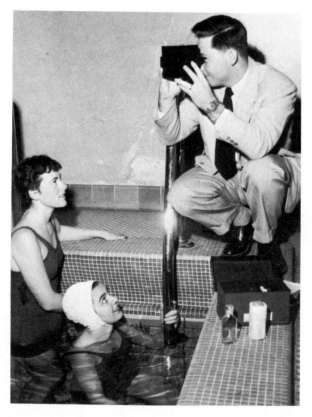

Fig. 27. Water quality in swimming or bathing waters is determined by the sanitarian measuring the concentration of disinfectant and the pH of the water. He will also collect a sample of water for laboratory analysis. Results from this testing will be used in giving advice or directions to the operator of the facilities.

one approach used by environmental sanitarians to achieve environmental control. Occasionally they must press for the enforcement of laws that define the basic sanitation standards that must be maintained.

Environmental sanitarians work in a wide variety of settings. In food processing and retailing establishments they work to ensure consumer protection from food-borne contamination. They work with private and public water and waste water disposal systems to check that the water supply is free from contamination and is being adequately treated and disinfected. (See Figs. 27 and 28.) In hospitals and nursing homes, sanitarians inspect housekeeping and isolation procedures, food service facilities and operations, ventilation, utilities, and use of space to determine that they are functioning in a manner that will enhance the health of patients and not pose additional threats to their recovery.

WHAT IS THE EDUCATIONAL BACKGROUND?

Educational programs are available in environmental sanitation at the associate, baccalaureate, and graduate degree levels. The

Fig. 28. The sanitarian may run bacteriological analyses of water samples and interpret the results when he has only a few samples and time is critical.

175

program of study combines liberal arts and technical studies that have many practical applications in environmental control and community health programs. The technical aspects of the program emphasize the natural and health sciences, preparing environmental sanitarians to evaluate and prescribe modifications of those environmental conditions that are detrimental to society or to prevent such problems from occurring. Studies in the humanities and social sciences orient prospective environmental sanitarians to the art of communication and help them to understand and relate to people, skills that are essential in obtaining environmental change. The "professional" portion of the curriculum includes a number of courses in environmental sanitation and industrial hygiene, microbiology, health education, epidemiology, health services administration, and biostatistics.

An increasing number of community colleges offer programs for those interested in becoming environmental health technicians. Graduates will have a background in the natural and social sciences plus specific training in environmental control techniques. They will be skilled in methods of observing and recording the sanitation standards that are essential in planning or modifying a control program. The environmental health technician works with and under the supervision of the environmental sanitarian.

Baccalaureate programs are offered through curricula in health and community education, life sciences, and allied health. There is a period of field training after graduation. Graduate study is a prerequisite for most advanced positions in administration and teaching. Students interested in these advanced positions may choose graduate programs in environmental health, public health, and other related sciences.

WHO IS THE REGISTERED SANITARIAN?

Registration laws are currently in force in thirty-four states. In several of these states, registration is voluntary, but in the remainder it is a requirement. To be eligible to take the registration examination, one must have a bachelor of science degree in environmental health or a closely related area that includes a background in the biological sciences. The examination consists of both written and oral sections. The National Environmental Health Association conducts a registration program for states that do not have their own, and the American Intersociety Academy for Certification of Sanitarians, Inc., also has a certification program. This Academy includes a variety of organizations that have represented sanitarians and have worked together to define professional requirements for the environmental sanitarian. Sanitarians with nine years of professional experience, an established record of accomplishment in the field, and a master's degree may be elected diplomates in the Academy.

WHAT ARE THE OPPORTUNITIES?

Sanitarians beginning their careers in the field of environmental health need general exposure and experience in working with the multiple facets of environmental sanitation and in working with and relating to people. Then they may specialize in a specific area such as institutional or hospital sanitation or in one of many other areas. At this stage in their professional development they must function as program planners and evaluators, supervisors of subprofessional personnel, and developers of standards and methods that will improve our environment. Sanitarians may develop professionally as specialists with great technical competence or as administrators. Many sanitarians do both.

The majority of employment opportunities are with local and state health agencies or food and drug agencies. Employment is also avaliable in health care institutions and industry, and there are some foreign assignments available.

Environmental sanitarians are the generalists in the field of environmental control and may be referred to as "environmentalists" or "environmental health specialists." As they specialize, their titles frequently change to reflect their areas of specialization. Industrial hygiene, radiology, hospital sanitation, and air or water pollution control are a few examples of such specialties. Not all persons working as specialists in these areas begin their careers as environmental sanitarians; in fact, they may have training only in a single area or function. Starting salaries range from $8,000 to $11,400 annually. Currently, the field is largely composed of men, but opportunities for women are increasing.

SUMMARY

Environmental sanitarians work with community institutions and with the general public to implement good sanitation practices and environmental control programs. Their goal is disease prevention and improvement in man's environment. Just as there has been an increased awareness of our environment and of the need for preserving it, there has been an increasing demand for environmental sanitation personnel. The field of environmental health is a dynamic, challenging field for those interested in both technology and working with people.

BIBLIOGRAPHY

Educational and other qualifications of public health sanitarians, Washington, D. C., 1956, American Public Health Association.

Hospital, a haven of health and how to keep it that way, Denver, 1965, National Environment Health Association.

Public health sanitarian, S.R.A. Occupational Brief No. 248, Chicago, 1968, Science Research Association, Inc.

Sanitarian series, G.S. 688, Washington, D. C., 1969, United States Civil Service Commission.

PROFESSIONAL ORGANIZATIONS WHERE FURTHER INFORMATION CAN BE OBTAINED:

National Environmental Health Association
1600 Pennsylvania Avenue
Denver, Colorado 80203

American Public Health Association
1015 18th Street N.W.
Washington, D. C. 20036

Chapter 22

EMERGING HEALTH PROFESSIONS

James P. Dearing

The Allied Health Professions Training Act of 1966 (Public Law 89-751), passed on November 3, 1966, gave federal recognition to a problem confronting all persons interested in the provision of health care. The terms of the act recognize two types of health care occupations and make funds available to develop and improve programs that train both types of personnel. The first category includes students seeking a baccalaureate degree (or its equivalent) or a master's degree who desire to meet basic professional requirements for employment as (1) medical technologists, (2) optometric technologists, (3) dental hygienists, (4) radiologic technologists, (5) medical records librarians, (6) dietitians, (7) occupational therapists, and (8) physical therapists.

The second category includes students working for an associate degree or its equivalent to qualify for employment as (1) x-ray technicians, (2) medical records technicians, (3) inhalation therapy technicians, (4) dental laboratory technicians, (5) dental hygienists, (6) dental assistants, (7) ophthalmic assistants, (8) occupational therapy technicians, (9) food service assistants, (10) medical technologists, and (11) optometric technologists. Thus the Allied Health Act recognizes eight allied health professions and an additional eleven areas of employment below the baccalaureate degree level of training. The latter list has been expanded greatly by numerous authors, and it is generally agreed that there are more than 250 discrete, definable health-related occupations in existence in this country today. What is it that allows some of these occupations to qualify as professions? By what process does a health occupation become a health profession? Which are now in the process of emerging as true allied health professions?

WHAT IS A PROFESSION?

The word "profession" is generally defined as work done skillfully for pay. When considering a more specific definition of the word as it applies to the allied health professions, it is generally conceded that a profession has several characteristics beyond those of the classic dictionary definition. Most descriptions of a profession in this sense include such elements as the following:

1. A profession is based upon a discrete, definable body of knowledge.
2. In the practice of a profession its members demonstrate skill based upon this knowledge and upon specific training in their profession.
3. A profession generally admits members and regulates internal mobility through a system of examinations, certification, or registration and establishes standards for the professional conduct of its members through the enforcement of a code of ethics.
4. A profession involves service for the well-being of mankind.

HOW DOES AN OCCUPATION BECOME A PROFESSION?

The histories of virtually all professions in existence today demonstrate that each profession developed through a relatively slow evolutionary process. A case in point is medical dietetics. Over an extended period of time a group of interested health professionals at The Ohio State University determined that there was a need to educate dietitians with an emphasis on pertinent medical aspects. A discrete body of knowledge was defined and training and teaching methods were developed. The approach is revolutionary in that clinical experience is initiated at the beginning of the third undergraduate year rather than during the year following graduation. This interest in combining the clinical with the didactic led in 1961 to the introduction of the medical dietetics curriculum at The Ohio State University. This program was the first of its kind in the country.

Another example of this process is the evolution of medical technology as a profession. At the end of World War I, pathologists first recognized a need for workers to assist them in the medical laboratory. In 1928 the American Society of Clinical Pathologists (ASCP) established the Board of Registry of Medical Technologists in order to standardize the training of laboratory workers, and by 1933 the American Society of Medical Technologists had been established. In 1949 the ASCP established the Board of Schools of Medical Technology. Members of the American Society of Medical Technologists are included on both the Board of Registry and Board of Schools. Although some programs leading to a baccalaureate degree in medical technology have existed for many years, a baccalaureate degree will be a requirement for certification for the first time in 1974. Thus medical technology has become an established profession within the last few years.

With the technological explosion that has continued since the beginning of World War II, it has become apparent that if we are to keep up with today's developments in modern medicine, we will no longer be able to permit professional development to continue at this relatively slow rate. However, this is not meant to imply that there can be any relaxation in the standards for assessing needs and priorities because the development of new programs is accelerated.

In order to demonstrate how needs for new health programs are defined, educational requirements are established, and curricula are developed, an important new health profession, circulation technology, is used in this chapter as an example of the many newly emerging professions.

CIRCULATION TECHNOLOGY—A NEW PROFESSION

Circulation technology is a new addition to the group of allied health professions. It was conceived of and developed at The Ohio State University in response to a demonstrable need that has been apparent since the late 1950s.

Since the first elective open heart operation supported by cardiopulmonary bypass was performed in 1953, there has been a remarkable growth of extracorporeal (outside the body) circulation technology. In 1968 there were more than 100,000 such operations performed in more than 1,000 institutions in this country alone. (See Fig. 29.) Concurrent with the first open heart procedures, hemodialysis (removal of waste from the blood via the artificial kidney) became an accepted treatment for patients suffering from kidney failure. (See Fig. 30.) There are now more than 204 hemodialysis centers registered with the Kidney Disease Control Program of the United States Public Health Service.

During the early developmental days of circulation technology the devices used were physician developed and physician operated. Gradually this responsibility has changed hands, as physicians recognized that it was an inefficient use of their time and that their medical training did not encompass the engineering skills required for continued development of the technology.

The first nonphysician operators of these devices were specially trained nurses, bioengineers, and physiologists. These highly edu-

Fig. 29. Preparation of the heart-lung machine that is used to provide circulatory support for patients undergoing open heart surgery requires meticulous attention to detail.

cated specialists soon found that the demands on their time were too great, and therefore the responsibility was further relegated to a corps of competent technicians. During the past several years it has become evident that the knowledge of these technicians has become diluted because they have been trained primarily by other technicians rather than by the physicians, bioengineers, and physiologists who trained the first technicians in this field. At present a great diversity of background and training is evident at the technician level.

It was because of the lack of well-qualified technologists that the School of Allied Medical Professions at The Ohio State University committed itself in the late 1960s to the development of a circulation technology curriculum and to the elevation of this occu-

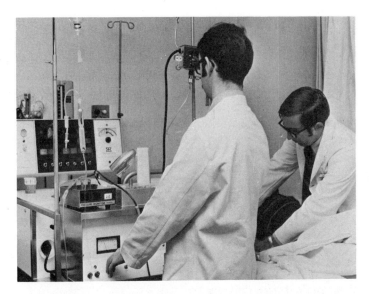

Fig. 30. Circulation technology students set up and operate the instrumentation for the renal dialysis of a patient.

pation to a professional status. The objective of the program is to provide a cadre of highly competent technologists, well-educated in both the biological and engineering aspects of extracorporeal circulation, who are able to provide the quality of service that good patient care demands.

Graduates of this program play a vital role in caring for those patients undergoing such procedures as heart/lung bypass for open heart surgery, circulatory support for the failing heart or lungs, removal of toxic products through the use of the artificial kidney, delivery of chemotherapeutic agents to the cancer patient, and a variety of diagnostic procedures. All of these techniques put the patient's circulatory system in direct continuity with instrumentation either for monitoring purposes or for the removal, processing, and subsequent return of the patient's blood to his own circulatory system.

Graduates are also able to function in a research capacity. Because their training includes components of both engineering and physiology, they will be able to provide an interface between physicians and engineers participating in the development of new circulation technology systems and methods.

183

Program development

In order to define that body of knowledge unique to the profession of circulation technology, a committee representing several disciplines—medicine, surgery, nursing, engineering, education, and biology—met with those who had organized the circulation technology program to establish the curriculum for this new division. Once this body of knowledge was defined, the committee discussed the most effective methods of presentation and evaluation and drew up course descriptions, syllabi, and lesson plans. At the same time efforts to select and equip physical facilities to house the developing program were initiated.

The permanent faculty that has been recruited represents both the biological and engineering sciences. Guest lecturers who contribute to the curriculum are drawn from many disciplines including engineering, medicine, veterinary medicine, education, and the biological sciences.

Baccalaureate degree program

Students spend two years at the preprofessional level at any accredited college or university, fulfilling the requirements for admission to the circulation technology division. These requirements include satisfactory completion of courses in biology, microbiology, mathematics, physics, chemistry, and English and sufficient credit hours to achieve junior standing.

Students are admitted to the program in the autumn quarter of their junior year. The two years of the circulation technology program include course work in pharmacology, general physiology, engineering fundamentals, aseptic environment, research methodology, and circulation technology instrumentation. In addition, there are courses in anatomy, physiology, and pathology as they relate specifically to circulation technology. Students in their senior year undertake a small research project of their own choice and are encouraged to work jointly with bioengineering students in collaborative research if such a project is feasible. Students who graduate from this program earn the degree of Bachelor of Science in Allied Health Professions.

Certificate program

A postbaccalaureate certificate program for selected students has been developed and approved by The Ohio State University. This program provides those with baccalaureate degrees in other fields the opportunity to receive the specialized training they will need in order to function as circulation technologists.

The prerequisites for admission to the certificate program include a baccalaureate degree from any accredited college or university, including satisfactory completion of the courses required for admission to the degree program, plus completion of additional courses in physiology, pharmacology, electrical engineering, and aseptic technique. Equivalency examinations are available for those courses unique to the program. Students are admitted during the summer quarters, and the program consists of four academic quarters in which the students are enrolled exclusively in special courses.

Professional organization

The American Society of Extracorporeal Technology was formed several years ago to bring together all persons interested in the field that we now define as circulation technology. Its membership is comprised of both heart/lung and dialysis technicians and technologists. The goals of the Society are to improve patient care by ensuring that practitioners meet certain standards of knowledge, proficiency, and professional conduct.

Concurrently with the development of the circulation technology curriculum at The Ohio State University, members of the American Society of Extracorporeal Technology have been actively engaged in converting this primarily technical society into a truly professional organization. During the annual meeting in 1970 a plan was submitted to the Board of Directors for the development of a registry for circulation technologists and for the establishment of an educational program that would incorporate the full body of knowledge that now defines the profession. This proposal calls for a registry comprised of several professional levels, with entrance to each based upon an individual's performance on a rigorous examination. Recommendations for the development of educational programs were primarily limited to the establishment of a list of essentials similar to those established by the AMA for other allied health professions. Minimal suggestions as to curricular content were contained in the educational proposal to allow the greatest latitude in the development of new programs.

Career opportunities in a new profession

It is already apparent that the demand for circulation technologists will for some time far surpass the supply of graduates available from one school. Graduates are being employed primarily in large medical centers where a variety of circulation technology procedures are carried out. Circulation technologists work to main-

Table 2. Emerging health professions*

Title of program	Institution	Stage of development
Child health (pediatric) associate	University of Colorado School of Medicine, 4200 E. Ninth Ave., Denver, Col.	Operational
Clinical associate	University of Texas Medical Branch, School of Medicine, Galveston, Texas	Operational
Clinical associate	Albert B. Chandler Medical Center School of Allied Health Professions, University of Kentucky, Lexington, Ky.	Planning
Corpsman	Cleveland Clinic Hospital, 2050 E. 93rd St., Cleveland, Ohio	Operational
"Medex"	Department of Preventive Medicine, School of Medicine, University of Washington, Seattle, Wash.	Operational
Nurse physician associate	Albert Einstein College of Medicine, 1300 Morris Park Ave., Bronx, N. Y.	Operational
Orthopedic assistant	City College of San Francisco, 50 Phelan Ave., San Francisco, Calif.	Operational
Orthopedic assistant	United States Public Health Service Hospital, Staten Island, N. Y.	Planning
Patient-care expeditor	Albert Einstein College of Medicine, 1300 Morris Park Ave., Bronx, N. Y.	Planning
Physician's assistant	Foothill College, 12345 El Monte Rd., Los Altos Hills, Calif.	Planning
Physician's assistant	Alderson-Broaddus College and Broaddus Hospital, Philippi, W. Va.	Operational
Physician's assistant program	Duke University Medical Center, Durham, N. C.	Operational

*From Kadish, J., and Long, J. W.: The training of physician assistants: status and issues, J.A.M.A. **212**:1047, 1970.

Table 2. Emerging health professions—cont'd

Title of program	Institution	Stage of development
Physician's assistant training program	Bowman Gray School of Medicine, Wake Forest University, Division of Allied Health Programs, Winston-Salem, N. C.	Operational
Physician assistant (with competencies in diabetes, oncology, gastroenterology, pediatrics, ophthalmology, neurosurgery, and general surgery)	Marshfield Clinic, Marshfield, Wis.	Planning
Physician assistant— surgical	Marshfield Clinic, Marshfield, Wis.	Operational
Purser-pharmacist mate course	Purser-Pharmacist Mate School, Public Health Service Hospital, Staten Island, N. Y.	Operational
Social worker aide	United States Public Health Service Hospital, Staten Island, N. Y.	Planning
Study of anesthesiology manpower problems for the development of new types of allied health personnel	Emory University School of Medicine, Atlanta, Ga.	Research
Triage or screening professional	Albert Einstein College of Medicine, 1300 Morris Park Ave., Bronx, N. Y.	Planning

tain quality control over these efforts both clinically and in the experimental laboratories. They also provide continuity in the delivery of these patient services by actually performing the services themselves or by training and supervising personnel to carry out such functions. Starting salaries in circulation technology vary from $8,000 to $12,000 annually, depending upon the amount of responsibility assumed and the services performed.

OTHER EMERGING HEALTH PROFESSIONS

Nineteen programs that were identified recently in the *Journal of the American Medical Association* train personnel who come under the general category of physician's assistants. These programs are presented in Table 2. Many of them are not yet operational, and many others have not yet graduated their first class. These programs are offered in a wide variety of educational settings, varying from private medical schools to two-year community colleges to medical facilities with no formal educational affiliations.

The requirements for admission to these programs are as varied as the educational environments in which they are conducted. Over half of the programs require previous experience in the health field, with nursing and the medical corps most often cited as being desirable. Some of these programs award baccalaureate or associate degrees, and others award certificates that acknowledge completion of the program.

Students graduating from these programs generally fall into one of the three categories of physician's assistants that were established by a committee of the National Academy of Sciences in a report to its membership. *Type A assistants* are capable of performing physical examinations, taking histories, and organizing data to help the physician diagnose the medical problem. They are also capable of assisting in the performance of various diagnostic and therapeutic procedures and in the coordination of total patient care. This physician's assistant is thus a medical generalist and may be called upon to exercise judgment.

Type B assistants are not trained as medical generalists; rather they possess in-depth knowledge in certain specialty areas. The circulation technologist described earlier in this chapter might well be classified as a type B assistant. *Type C assistants* are able to perform many tasks of a general nature, but because they do not possess in-depth medical knowledge, they will always work under the direct supervision of a physician.

Those programs that have placed graduates in the field have issued preliminary encouraging reports as to the acceptability and applicability of the educational programs.

Concurrent with the development of the programs listed in Table 2, an effort is underway to meet some of the other criteria of a profession through the creation of the American Association of Physician's Assistants. Current projects being undertaken by this group include the development of a continuing education program in cooperation with the Duke University Physician's Assistants program, and the investigation of the legal status of physician's assistants in the fifty states.

SUMMARY

The transformation of a health occupation into a health profession has been discussed and the historical evolution of several recognized allied health professions briefly described. The use of circulation technology as a model has demonstrated how a health occupation may be transformed into a health profession in this day of rapidly accelerating technology. Finally, an attempt has been made to show some of the innovative programs being developed today, with primary emphasis on the growth and development of the physician's assistant programs.

PROFESSIONAL ORGANIZATIONS WHERE FURTHER INFORMATION CAN BE OBTAINED:

American Association of Physician's Assistants
Box 2951 West Durham Station
Durham, North Carolina 27705

American Society of Extracorporeal Technology
287 East 6th Street
Saint Paul, Minnesota 55101

APPENDIX A

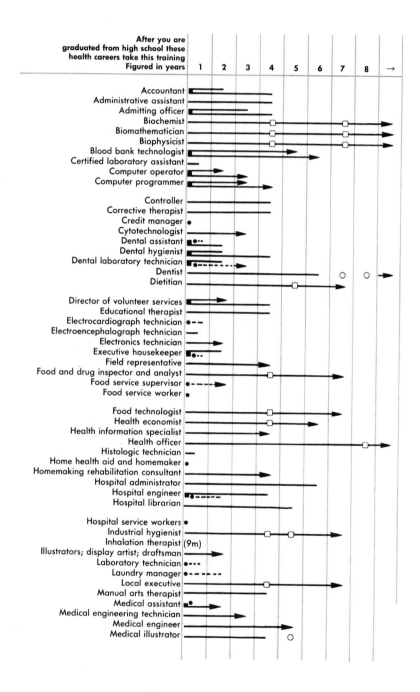

After you are graduated from high school these health careers take this training Figured in years

	1	2	3	4	5	6	7	8	→
Accountant									
Administrative assistant									
Admitting officer									
Biochemist									
Biomathematician									
Biophysicist									
Blood bank technologist									
Certified laboratory assistant									
Computer operator									
Computer programmer									
Controller									
Corrective therapist									
Credit manager									
Cytotechnologist									
Dental assistant									
Dental hygienist									
Dental laboratory technician									
Dentist									
Dietitian									
Director of volunteer services									
Educational therapist									
Electrocardiograph technician									
Electroencephalograph technician									
Electronics technician									
Executive housekeeper									
Field representative									
Food and drug inspector and analyst									
Food service supervisor									
Food service worker									
Food technologist									
Health economist									
Health information specialist									
Health officer									
Histologic technician									
Home health aid and homemaker									
Homemaking rehabilitation consultant									
Hospital administrator									
Hospital engineer									
Hospital librarian									
Hospital service workers									
Industrial hygienist									
Inhalation therapist	(9m)								
Illustrators; display artist; draftsman									
Laboratory technician									
Laundry manager									
Local executive									
Manual arts therapist									
Medical assistant									
Medical engineering technician									
Medical engineer									
Medical illustrator									

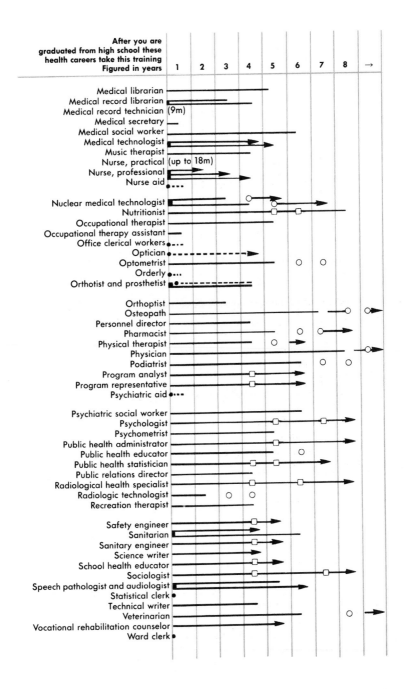

After you are graduated from high school these health careers take this training Figured in years

	1	2	3	4	5	6	7	8	→

Medical librarian
Medical record librarian
Medical record technician (9m)
Medical secretary
Medical social worker
Medical technologist
Music therapist
Nurse, practical (up to 18m)
Nurse, professional
Nurse aid

Nuclear medical technologist
Nutritionist
Occupational therapist
Occupational therapy assistant
Office clerical workers
Optician
Optometrist
Orderly
Orthotist and prosthetist

Orthoptist
Osteopath
Personnel director
Pharmacist
Physical therapist
Physician
Podiatrist
Program analyst
Program representative
Psychiatric aid

Psychiatric social worker
Psychologist
Psychometrist
Public health administrator
Public health educator
Public health statistician
Public relations director
Radiological health specialist
Radiologic technologist
Recreation therapist

Safety engineer
Sanitarian
Sanitary engineer
Science writer
School health educator
Sociologist
Speech pathologist and audiologist
Statistical clerk
Technical writer
Veterinarian
Vocational rehabilitation counselor
Ward clerk

APPENDIX B

Further information may be obtained from the following professional organizations:

American Association for Inhalation Therapy
3554 9th Street
Riverside, California 92501

American Association of Medical Record Librarians
211 East Chicago Avenue
Chicago, Illinois 60611

American Association of Nurse Anesthetists
3010 Prudential Plaza
Chicago, Illinois 60601

American Association of Physician's Assistants
Box 2951 West Durham Station
Durham, North Carolina 27705

American College of Hospital Administrators
840 North Lake Shore Drive
Chicago, Illinois 60611

American Dental Association and American Dental Hygienists Association
211 East Chicago Avenue
Chicago, Illinois 60611

American Dietetic Association
620 North Michigan Avenue
Chicago, Illinois 60611

American Medical Association
535 North Dearborn Street
Chicago, Illinois 60610

American Medical Record Association
875 North Michigan Avenue
Suite 1850 John Hancock Center
Chicago, Illinois 60611

American Nurses' Association
10 Columbus Circle
New York, New York 10019

American Occupational Therapy Association
251 Park Avenue South
New York, New York 10010

American Optometric Association
7000 Chippewa Street
St. Louis, Missouri 63119

American Pharmaceutical Association
2215 Constitution Avenue, N.W.
Washington, D. C. 20037

American Physical Therapy Association
1156 15th Street, N.W.
Washington, D. C. 20005

American Public Health Association
1015 18th Street, N.W.
Washington, D. C. 20036

American Registry of Inhalation Therapists, Inc.
c/o University of Rochester
School of Medicine
Rochester, New York 14620

American Registry of Radiologic Technologists
2600 Wayzata Boulevard
Minneapolis, Minnesota 55405

American Society of Clinical Pathologists
710 South Wolcott Avenue
Chicago, Illinois 60612

American Society of Extracorporeal Technology
287 East 6th Street
St. Paul, Minnesota 55101

American Society of Medical Technologists
Suite 1600 Hermann Professional Building
Houston, Texas 77025

American Society of Radiologic Technologists
645 North Michigan Avenue
Chicago, Illinois 60611

American Speech and Hearing Association
9030 Old Georgetown Road
Washington, D. C. 20014

American Veterinary Medical Association
600 South Michigan Avenue
Chicago, Illinois 60605

Association of Medical Illustrators
c/o Octavia Garlington
Medical Art Services
Medical College of Georgia
Augusta, Georgia 30904

Association of Schools of Allied Health Professions
#1 Dupont Circle
Suite 300
Washington, D. C. 20036

Association of University Programs in Hospital Administration
#1 Dupont Circle
Suite 420
Washington, D. C. 20036

Council on Social Work Education
345 East 46th Street
New York, New York 10017

National Association for Practical Nurse Education and Services
475 Riverside Drive
New York, New York 10027

National Association of Licensed Practical Nurses
250 West 57th Street
New York, New York 10019

National Association of Social Workers, Inc.
2 Park Avenue
New York, New York 10016

National Commission for Social Work Careers
345 East 46th Street
New York, New York 10017

National Environmental Health Association
1600 Pennsylvania Avenue
Denver, Colorado 80203

National Federation of Licensed Practical Nurses
250 West 57th Street
New York, New York 10019

National League for Nursing
10 Columbus Circle
New York, New York 10019

APPENDIX C

Professional education and manpower supply*

	Number of schools	Total annual enrollment	Total annual graduates	Number of active professionals
Nursing	1,287	145,588	41,555	680,000
Medicine	85	34,920	8,059	300,000
Pharmacy	74	15,097	4,500	124,460
Dentistry	53	16,008	3,433	102,000
Radiologic technology	1,175	12,031	5,481	60,982
Social work	67	12,551	5,060	52,000
Medical technology	789	4,000	4,000	35,000
Optometry	11	2,484	472	18,000
Dietetics	70	824	814	14,523
Veterinary medicine	21	5,471	1,318	13,532
Speech and hearing science	202	5,709	5,000	13,000
Physical therapy	52	3,011	1,347	13,000
Dental hygiene	74	5,931	2,231	9,200
Occupational therapy	37	3,128	907	9,126
Medical record administration	26	250	237	3,700
Inhalation therapy	79	385	145	1,150
Medical illustration	7	50	20	250 to 300

*The information contained in this table is based on data supplied by the national organizations. Numbers in the last column refer only to those at the professional level; they do not include supportive personnel.

APPENDIX D

Estimated persons employed in selected occupations in 1967*

Health field and occupation	Workers
Total	**3,375,300 to 3,410,600**
Administrator, program representative	39,000 to 44,000
Anthropologist—cultural and physical	600
Sociologist—medical	400
Systems analyst	500
Research scientist	52,000
Biomedical engineer	3,000
Biomedical engineering technician	6,000
Chiropractor, naturopath	16,000 to 18,000
Clinical laboratory services	100,000
Dentist	98,700
Dental hygienist	15,000
Dental assistant	95,000
Dental laboratory technician	27,000
Dietitian and nutritionist	30,000
Dietary technician, food service supervisor	6,000
Economist, health	500 to 600
Environmental engineer	9,000
Industrial hygienist	2,300
Other environmental program specialists	8,700
Sanitarian and sanitarian technician	15,000
Food technologist	20,000
Food-and-drug analyst and inspector	1,500
Health statistician, vital-record registrar, demographer	2,400
Public health educator	1,800
School health educator, coordinator	18,000
Health information specialist and science writer	2,000
Health technical writer	2,000

*From Turner, C. E.: Personal and community health, ed. 14, St. Louis, 1971, The C. V. Mosby Co.

Estimated persons employed in selected occupations in 1967 —cont'd

Health field and occupation	Workers
Total	**3,375,300 to 3,410,600**
Medical illustrator	500
Medical librarian	3,000
Medical library assistant	5,000
Medical record librarian	12,000
Medical record technician	25,000
Physician (M.D.)	294,100
Physician (D.O.)	11,400
Lay midwife	4,700
Registered nurse	659,000
Practical nurse	320,000
Nursing aide, orderly, attendant	800,000
Home health aide	12,000
Occupational therapist	11,000 to 12,000
Orthotist and prosthetist	3,500
Pharmacist	122,400
Pharmacy aide	5,600
Physical therapist	13,000
Physical therapy assistant, aide	6,000 to 8,000
Podiatrist	8,000
Psychologist	9,000
Radiologic (x-ray) technologist, technician	75,000 to 100,000
Secretary, office assistant	250,000
Social work (clinical)	21,700
Therapist (specialized rehabilitation)	8,600 to 8,800
Speech pathologist and audiologist	16,000
Veterinarian	24,200
Optometrist	17,000
Optician	8,000
Vision care technician	15,000
Orthoptist	400
Vocational rehabilitation counselor	7,800
Miscellaneous health services	34,000

INDEX

A

Accreditation of health education programs, 6
Accrediting, National Commission on, 6
Air, dephlogisticated, 95-96
Allied Health Professions Training Act, 179
American Association for Inhalation Therapy (AAIT), 96
American Association of Nurse Anesthetists (AANA), 54
American College of Hospital Administrators, 151-152
American Dental Association (ADA), 23-24, 79
American Dietetic Association, 87
American Medical Association (AMA), 6
American Medical Record Association (AMRA), 106
American Occupational Therapy Association (AOTA), 123
American Optometric Association (AOA), 33
American Physical Therapy Association (APTA), 71
American Society of Extracorporeal Technology, 185
American Society of Medical Technologists (ASMT), 110, 180
American Society of Radiologic Technologists (ASRT), 132
American Speech and Hearing Association, 139
Anemia, definition of, 112
Anesthesia, spinal, development of, 41
Anesthesiology, nurse, 53-56

Anesthesiology, nurse—cont'd
education in, 56
personal qualities in, 56
professional development of, 54
responsibilities of, 54-56
Aniseikonia, definition of, 32
Aristotle, 95
Assistants, physician's, 186-189
Audiologist; see Speech and hearing science
Audiovisuals, 162

B

Baltimore College of Dental Surgery, 22
Banting, Frederick, 12
Beaumont, William, 11
Beddoes, Thomas, 96
Bell, Alexander Graham, 136-137
Best, Charles, 12
Bilirubin, definition of, 114
Binocular coordination, definition of, 31
Black, G. V., 22-23
Boher, John, 22
Boyle, Robert, 95
Brödel, Max, 168
Brucellosis, 37

C

Career choices in medicine, 16-18
Certification of health care personnel, 6-7
de Chauliac, Guy, 21
Circulation technology, 181-187
career opportunities in, 185-187
educational requirements of, 184-185
history of, 181-184

Circulation technology—cont'd
organization of, 185
Colt, Samuel, 96
Communications, medical, 158-166
educational program in, 160-161
history of, 159-160
professionals in,
contributing, 162-164
specialists in, 161-162
Communication factors of health
care education, 3
Community health nursing, 51
Cytology, definition of, 116
Cytotechnologists, 116-117

D

De Humani Corporis Fabrica, 167
Dental assistant, 25-26
Dental Association, American
(ADA), 23-24, 79
Dental hygiene, 79-84
background of, 79
education in, 79-81
functions of and career
opportunities in, 82-83
licensing in, 82
personal qualifications in, 83
professional organizations
of, 83
Dental hygienists, 25; *see also*
Dental hygiene
Dental laboratory technicians, 25
Dentatores, 21
Dentistry, 21-28
careers in, 26-27
education in, 23-24
future trends of, 26
history of, 21-23
personal qualifications in, 27
supporting professionals
in, 24-26
Dephlogisticated air, 95-96
Diagnostic radiology, 128-131
Dietetic Association,
American, 87
Dietetics, 85-94
development of, 85-87
dietitian, registered, 89-90
educational preparation
in, 87-89
job opportunities in, 90-92
medical, 180
need for, 92
supporting professionals
in, 92-93
Doctor of Optometry (O.D.), 33

Doctor of Veterinary Medicine
(D.V.M.), 43
Drugs, prescription, and
community pharmacists, 65-66
D.V.M. degree, 43

E

Ebers papyrus, 64, 85
Economic factors of health care
education, 2-3
Ellis, Alexander J., 137
Environmental Health
Association, National, 176-177
Environmental sanitation,
173-178
educational background
of, 175-176
functions of, 174-175
history of, 173-174
opportunities in, 177
registered sanitarian, 176-177
Extracorporeal, definition of, 181
Extracorporeal Technology,
American Society of, 185

F

Fauchard, Pierre, 22
Fleming, Alexander, 12
Fletcher, Harvey, 137
Flexner, Abraham, 13
Fluoridation of water supplies,
resistance to, 3
Fones, Alfred C., 79

G

Galen; *see* Galenus, Claudius
Galenus, Claudius, 9
Government, health care
education and, 5
Greenwood, John, 22

H

Harris, Chapin B., 22
Harris, John, 22
Harvey, William, 10
Health agencies, voluntary,
growth of, 4
Health care
laws on, 5
necessity of, public attitude
toward, 3
nurse-midwifery contributions
to, 57-58
nurses' contribution to, 48

Health care—cont'd
  personnel in, licensing,
    certification, and registration
    of, 6-7
  physical therapists'
    contribution to, 72-74
  professionals in, education
    of, 1-8
    accreditation of health
      education programs, 6
    licensing, certification, and
      registration of, 6-7
  team concept in, 1-2
Health care education, 1-8
Health careers, calendar
  of, 191-193
Health education, programs for,
  accreditation of, 6
Health Manpower Act, 5
Health professions, emerging,
  179-189
  circulation technology, 181-187
  occupation becomes
    profession, 180-181
  profession, definition of,
    179-180
Health Professions Training Act,
  Allied, 179
Health services, administration
  of; see Hospital and health
  services administration
Health team, 1-2
Hearing Association, American
  Speech and, 139
Hearing science, speech and,
  135-143
  definition of, 135-136
  history of, 136-137
  need for, 138
  study of, 138-143
  voice communication,
    adequate, 137-138
Helmholtz, Herman, 137
Helping the Dying Patient and
  His Family, 147-148
Hematology, medical
  technologists in, 111-112
Hemodialysis, definition of, 181
Hemophilia, definition of, 112
Hill-Burton Act, 5
Hippocrates, 9
Histologic technicians, 117
Holmes, Oliver Wendell, 11
Hooke, Robert, 95
Hospital Administrators,
  American College of, 151-152

Hospital and health services
  administration, 151-157
  educational preparation in,
    152-153
  history of, 151-152
  need for, 156-157
  personal qualities in, 153
  professionals in, related,
    153-156
Hospital pharmacies, 67-68
Hospitals, public attitude
  toward, 4
Hunter, John, 22

I

Illustration, medical, 162, 167-172
  career opportunities in, 171
  educational requirements in,
    168-169
  history of, 167-168
  professional, 169-171
Inhalation therapy, 95-102
  history of, 95-98
  professional levels and
    education in, 100-101
  professional services of, scope
    of, 98-100
Inhalation Therapy, American
  Association for (AAIT), 96
Insulin, discovery of, 12
Internship, 14

J

Jenner, Edward, 10-11

K

Kalkar, Jan Stephan, 167
Kelly, Howard, 168
Kennedy, Nathalie, 147-148
Kilbourne, F. L., 37-38

L

Laboratory technicians, dental, 25
Lavoisier, Antoine, 85-95
Laws
  on health care, 5
  malpractice, disadvantage of, 7
Leukemia, definition of, 112
Librarians, medical, 162
Licensed practical nursing, 59-62
  education in, 60-61
  employment opportunities in,
    62
  licensure in, 61

Licensed practical nursing—cont'd
preenrollment requirements in,
60
role of, 61-62
training available in, 59-60
Licensing of health care
personnel, 6-7
Ligation, definition of, 10
Lister, Joseph, 11
Logopedists; see Speech and
hearing science
Long, Crawford, 11

M

Malpractice law, disadvantage
of, 7
Medicaid, 5
Medical communications, 158-166
educational program in, 160-161
history of, 159-160
professionals in, contributing,
162-164
specialists in, 161-162
Medical illustration, 162, 167-172
career opportunities in, 171
educational requirements in,
168-169
history of, 167-168
professional, 169-171
Medical issues of our time, 19-20
Medical librarians, 162
Medical Programs, Regional, 5
Medical record administration,
103-108
educational requirements in,
106-107
job opportunities in, 107
medical records, 103-105
personal qualities in, 107
professional status of, 107
role of, 105-106
supportive personnel in,
107-108
Medical Record Association,
American (AMRA), 106
Medical school, admission to,
nonscholastic requirements in,
15-17
Medical School Admission
Requirements U.S.A. and
Canada, 15
Medical social work, 144-150
career opportunities in, 149
development of, 144-145
educational requirements in,
145-146

Medical social work—cont'd
functions of, 146-148
Medical Technologists, American
Society of (ASMT), 110, 180
Medical technology, 109-118,
180-181
demand for, 117-118
development of, 109-110
educational requirements in,
114-116
job opportunities in, 110-114
salaries in, 117
supporting professionals for,
116-117
Medicare, 5
Medicine, 9-20
career choices in, 16-18
education in, 13-17
admission to school, 15-17
costs of, 14-15
development of, 13
today, 13-14
medical issues of our time,
19-20
nuclear, 131-132
physician, activities of, 18
practice, method of, 18-19
professional development of,
9-12
veterinary, 36-46
education in, 42-43
history of, 36
job opportunities in, 44-46
licensure requirements in, 43
supportive personnel in, 46
today, 36-42
Microbiology, medical
technologists in, 110
Midwifery; see Nurse-midwifery
Morgan, Charles, 13
Morton, William, 11
Morton, W. G. T., 22

N

National Association of Social
Workers, 149
National Environmental Health
Association, 176-177
National Institutes of Health, 5
National League for Nursing
(NLN), 50
New England Hospital for
Women and Children, 47
Nightingale, Florence, 47
Nuclear medicine, 131-132
Nurse, definition of, 47

Nurse anesthesiology, 53-56
  education in, 56
  personal qualities in, 56
  professional development of, 54
  responsibilities of, 54-56
Nurse Anesthetists, American
  Association of (AANA), 54
Nurse-midwifery, 56-59
  health care contributions of,
    57-58
  history of, 58-59
  role of, 57
Nursing
  community health, 51
  National League for (NLN), 50
  practical, licensed, 59-62
    education in, 60-61
    employment opportunities
      in, 62
    licensure of, 61
    preenrollment requirements
      in, 60
    role of, 61-62
    training available in, 59-60
  psychiatric, 51
  registered, 47-53
    education in, 49-50
    health care contributions of,
      48
    history of, 47-48
    job opportunities in, 50-52
    need for, 53
  related programs, 47-63
    nurse anesthesiology, 53-56
    nurse-midwifery, 56-59
    practical nursing, licensed,
      59-62
    registered nursing, 47-53

O

Obstetrics, definition of, 58
Occupational therapy, 119-126
  functions of, 119-123
  history of, 119
  opportunities in, professional,
    125-126
  organization of, professional,
    125
  personnel levels in, 123-125
Occupational Therapy
  Association, American
  (AOTA), 123
O.D. degree, 33
Optometric assistants, 33-34
Optometric Association,
  American (AOA), 33

Optometric technicians, 34
Optometry, 29-35
  careers in, 32
  education in, 33
  future outlook of, 34-35
  optometric assistants, 33-34
  personal qualities in, 32-33
  professional development of, 29
  professional functions of, 30-31
Oxygen, effect of, 95-96

P

Paget, Sir Richard, 137
Parasitology, medical
  technologists in, 110
Paré, Ambroise, 10
Penicillin, discovery of, 12
Pharmacies, hospital, 67-68
Pharmacists, community
  functions of, 66-67
  and prescription drugs, 65-66
Pharmacy, 64-70
  career opportunities in, 68
  education in, 69-70
  salaries in, starting, 69
  women in, 69
Phonetician, definition of, 136
Phoniatrist; see Speech and
  hearing science
Physical therapy, 71-78
  education in, 74-75
  employment opportunities in,
    76-77
  health care contribution of,
    72-74
  history of, 71-72
  professional qualities in, 75
  statistics, current, 77-78
  supportive personnel in, 76
Physical Therapy Association,
  American (APTA), 71
Physician; see also Medicine
  activities of, 18
  practice of, 18-19
Physician's assistants, 186-189
Physiology, history of, 10
Pneumatic Institute, 96
Political factors in health care
  education, 5
Practical nursing, 59-62
  education in, 60-61
  employment opportunities in,
    62
  licensure in, 61
  preenrollment requirements
    in, 60

Practical nursing—cont'd
  role of, 61-62
  training available in, 59-60
Practice of physician, method
  of, 18-19
Prescription drugs, community
  pharmacists and, 65-66
Priestley, Joseph, 95-96
Profession, definition of, 179-180
Psychiatric nursing, 51

R

Rabies control, 37
Radiologic Technologists,
  American Society of (ASRT),
  132
Radiologic technology, 127-134
  development of, 127-128
  educational preparation in,
    132-133
  nuclear medicine, 131-132
Radiology
  diagnostic, 128-131
  therapeutic, 131
Reconstruction aides;
  see Physical therapy
Reed, Walter, 38
Regional Medical Programs, 5
Registered nursing, 47-53
  education in, 49-50
  health care contributions of, 48
  history of, 47-48
  job opportunities in, 50-52
  need for, 53
Registration of health care
  personnel, 6-7
Rehabilitation Act, Vocational, 5
Residency, 14
Roentgen, Wilhelm Konrad, 12
Rush, Benjamin, 36

S

Sanitation, environmental,
  173-178
  educational background in,
    175-176
  functions of, 174-175
  history of, 173-174
  opportunities in, 177
  registered sanitarian, 176-177
Santi, Raffaello, 167
Scientific factors in health care
  education, 4-5
Scripture, Edward, 137
Semmelweis, Ignaz, 11

Sensation of Tone, 137
Serology, medical technologists
  in, 110-111
Sigma Phi Alpha, 83
Smith, Theobald, 37-38
Social Security Act, Medicare
  and Medicaid addition to, 5
Social work, medical, 144-150
  career opportunities in, 149
  development of, 144-145
  educational requirements in,
    145-146
  functions of, 146-148
Social Workers, National
  Association of, 149
Sociological factors in health
  care education, 3-4
Speech and Hearing Association,
  American, 139
Speech and hearing science,
  135-143
  definition of, 135-136
  history of, 136-137
  need for, 138
  study of, 138-143
  voice communication,
    adequate, 137-138
Spinal anesthesia, development
  of, 41
Stader, Otto, 41
Stader splint, 41
Substitution therapy and
  medicine, effect of, 4

T

Taylor, James, 22
Team concept in health care, 1-2
Technological factors of health
  care education, 5-6
Terry, Luther, 40
Therapeutic radiology, 131
Therapy
  inhalation, 95-102
    history of, 95-98
    professional levels and
      education in, 100-101
    professional services of,
      scope of, 98-100
  occupational, 119-126
    functions of, 119-123
    history of, 119
    opportunities in,
      professional, 125-126
    organization of,
      professional, 125
    personnel levels in, 123-125

Therapy—cont'd
  physical, 71-78
    education of, 74-75
    employment opportunities
      in, 76-77
    health care contributions of,
      72-74
    history of, 71-72
    professional qualities in, 75
    statistics, current, 77-78
    supportive personnel in, 76
  substitution, effect of on
    medicine, 4
Treatment, focus of, 6

U

University of Pennsylvania
  Medical School, 13

V

Vaccination, discovery of, 10-11
Vectors, definition of, 38

Vesalius, Andreas, 9, 95, 165
Veterinary medicine, 36-46
  education in, 42-43
  history of, 36
  job opportunities in, 44-46
  licensure requirements in, 43
  supportive personnel in, 46
  today, 36-42
da Vinci, Leonardo, 167
Vocational Rehabilitation Act, 5
Voice communication, 137-138
Voluntary health agencies,
  growth of, 4

W

Walter Reed Army Hospital, 71
Water supply fluoridation,
  resistance to, 3
Wells, Horace, 22

Z

Zoonoses, definition of, 37